The COMPLETE BOOK OF PORK

BUTCHERING, SMOKING, CURING, SAUSAGE MAKING, and COOKING

The COMPLETE BOOK of PORK

BUTCHERING, SMOKING, CURING, SAUSAGE MAKING, and COOKING

PHILIP HASHEIDER

Voyageur
Press

Quarto is the authority on a wide range of topics.

Quarto educates, entertains and enriches the lives of our readers—enthusiasts and lovers of hands-on living.

www.quartoknows.com

First published in 2016 by Voyageur Press, an imprint of Quarto Publishing Group USA Inc., 400 First Avenue North, Suite 400, Minneapolis, MN 55401 USA. Telephone: (612) 344-8100 Fax: (612) 344-8692

quartoknows.com
Visit our blogs at quartoknows.com

Voyageur Press titles are also available at discounts in bulk quantity for industrial or sales-promotional use. For details contact the Special Sales Manager at Quarto Publishing Group USA Inc., 400 First Avenue North, Suite 400, Minneapolis, MN 55401 USA.

10 9 8 7 6 5 4 3 2 1

ISBN: 978-0-7603-4996-0

Acquiring Editor: Todd R. Berger
Project Manager: Caitlin Fultz
Art Director: Brad Springer
Cover Designer: Rob Johnson
Layout: Danielle Smith-Boldt

Printed in China

DEDICATION

This book is dedicated to my brother, Bruce Hasheider, whose lifelong interest in pork production has served as an encouragement and inspiration for hundreds of 4-H and FFA members across Wisconsin, and programs that he has supported for many years.

CONTENTS

Raising a pig from a very young age to butchering weight can be a rewarding experience by itself and one in which your entire family can participate.

INTRODUCTION

The local food movement has been gaining in popularity in recent years as consumers have become more aware of where their food is produced, under what conditions it is produced—such as humanely, organically, or conventionally—or the distance it travels to reach a market where they shop. This has led many to try their hand at raising live animals to then butcher them and process the meat for family use. Whether these animals are cows, goats, chickens, turkeys, sheep, or pigs, this back-to-the-farm approach is seen as a way to ensure animals are raised in ways that conform to that family's ideals and values, besides being an activity in which all members, whether young or old, can participate.

This book focuses on one farm animal species—the pig—and how to raise it, butcher it, process the resulting carcass, and preserve the meat. It offers recipes to use virtually every part of the animal. It is the goal of this discussion to use every portion of the pig, except perhaps its "oink." And that is the best way to honor the animal—by using every possible part without wasting anything. Some parts of the pig will have multiple uses while other parts may have more limited ones.

Who, then, is this book for? And what will it provide?

The range of people who will glean useful information from this book can include lifestyle country farmers, urban food enthusiasts, and anyone with a determination to provide food for their family. What at first may seem an insurmountable task will be broken down into easily manageable sections that will explain all the processes involved.

Within the following pages, you will find reliable information about all the issues involved from start to finish: from securing and raising a small pig to it becoming a large animal intended for harvest.

You will learn how to safely and humanely raise that pig, dispatch a live animal, the steps required to deconstruct a carcass into useful portions, and the ways to preserve the meat, whether it is in standard cuts or made into sausage.

You can use the recipes included as a starting point for developing different family meals and learn about a variety of ways to use each cut and methods of preparation.

Meat preservation is an important aspect of any butchering program because you will be unlikely to use all of the fresh meat immediately. We will examine what preservation process may work best for different cuts and any alternatives. And you will learn how these cuts can fit into your and your family's diets with the numerous recipes found throughout this book. This may sound like an ambitious task, but the rewards of reading this book will more than make up for the time you spend with it.

We'll begin by briefly reviewing the history of the pig in America. Porcine history, or the story of pigs, dates back 40 million years to fossils found of wild piglike animals that roamed ancient forests and swamps in present-day Europe and Asia. China began domesticating pigs about 7,000 years ago, and they were being raised in Europe 3,500 years ago. History records that Christopher Columbus took eight pigs with him to Cuba in 1493. In 1539, Hernando de Soto landed in southern Florida with thirteen pigs, and that gave birth to America's pork industry.

In the following three hundred years, the pig population—both domesticated and feral (those that escaped captivity and developed in the wild, the "razorbacks")—expanded as the migration of pioneers moved westward from the eastern seaboard states. In its early rural history, Manhattan Island was home to many colonists' pigs. It reached the point where a solid wall was built on the north edge of the colony—today's Wall Street—to control roaming herds of pigs.

With their western migration, settlers took pigs along as a source of food as they settled new areas. The pigs' rapid rate of growth, the diverse products derived from one pig, and the large numbers of offspring that could be produced from one female made pigs an early source of wealth and health. These three qualities are still very much in evidence today for those who raise pigs.

Today, pork is probably more popular than ever before. It is outpacing all other proteins in the food service industry. This increase is in all aspects of pork, fresh or processed, with a large demand for ham, breakfast sausages, and bacon.

This increased popularity is partly due to promotion from food service businesses, which have added pork items across the day and evening menus rather than focusing only on breakfast entrees. It is also due to the increasing awareness and consumer recognition of the healthful aspects of pork.

Besides having a desirable taste, pork is a nutritious meat, is easy to prepare, and can be offered at every meal. Pork is a lean protein, and in 2005 the United States Department of Agriculture (USDA) presented a study that stated that six common cuts of fresh pork are leaner today than fifteen years ago and are on average about 16 percent lower in total fat and 27 percent lower in saturated fat. Also, when compared to a skinless chicken breast, pork tenderloin is now just as lean. Pork is now popular for diet-conscious consumers.

The decrease in fat within the muscle has caused slight changes in how pork is grilled, baked, braised, or broiled, because with less fat interlaced within the muscles, the meat cooks faster. This shift in the components of pork muscle has a beneficial health aspect for you and your family. You can retain the flavor while lowering your fat intake. Choosing pork as a menu item can add variety to your home meals as well as a good protein source.

One advantage to raising and processing your own pork is that you can decrease the overall cost of the meat when compared to purchasing it at the store counter. Also, you know how your animal was raised, what you fed it, how it was treated, and a host of intangibles that you can't get elsewhere, such as working with a live animal.

A recent study made by the University of Wisconsin-Extension swine team shows that during the past three censuses, the small pig producer who sells one to twenty-four animals a year is one of the fastest-growing segments of agriculture. You will be in good company.

You do not have to raise a pig to have access to pork meat. They can be purchased fully grown from local pig producers.

Chapter 1
RAISING YOUR OWN PIG

Developing a plan is the first step before setting out to purchase a pig to raise. Unexpected problems can often be avoided by having thought through all the steps that are required to raise a small piglet to one ready to butcher.

There is no sidestepping the obvious fact that small pigs grow up into large pigs if fed well. At that point you will need to decide, if you have avoided it all along, whether to let the animal live out its life in the area you house it, sell it to market to recover your costs, or use it to fill your freezer.

Let's assume you decide to butcher the animal that you will raise or you wouldn't be reading this book. How do you get there in the first place? This chapter will provide the basics of how to provide adequate housing and enclosures, select and purchase a pig, and raise and feed it, and it covers issues involving general swine husbandry. You are about to become a successful small-scale farmer. But first, some caveats.

FACILITIES AND HOUSING

Before we dive into the process of buying a pig, you will need to set up a place for it to live once you bring it home and for the time you raise it. Housing is required for most small-farming situations where livestock are involved. Whether to provide shelter from heat, wind, snow, ice, or cold, livestock need protection at times just as humans do. While animals are quite resilient on their own, you will need to provide space for them to minimize risk relating to temperature and weather variations.

You should have a living space selected before you bring a pig home. Most pigs adapt quickly to new surroundings if they have a comfortable bed, fresh water, and plenty of food.

The number of pigs you plan to raise at one time will influence the type and size of their housing needs. Having more than one pig will require more space if several are involved. For our discussion, let's assume you are buying two small pigs to raise.

The reason for two rather than one pig is that pigs are very social animals and they do better if they have a companion. Yes, they will scrap and play and even ignore each other from time to time, just like little kids. And they will continue to do so even as they get older. This is natural behavior for them, and to deprive them of social interaction with another pig means you may have to become their substitute companion by spending time with them.

You may be able to substitute a second pig with a cow, sheep, or goat as a companion animal, but having another pig about the same size will allow them to socialize. Because many of our following housing and feeding calculations are made for a single pig, you will need to double them to account for the second one.

One pig weighing between 10 to 40 pounds will typically require about 4 square feet of space to be comfortable. As they approach 150 pounds in weight, the space increases to about 7 square feet each. Larger pigs weighing 200 pounds or more, or pregnant females (sows), require about 15 square feet. But this is close confinement. A larger space is better and you should plan for a minimum of 200 square feet or more for indoor comfort. Having a small pasture or lot where the pig can go out to exercise or roam about will offer more room. However, the internal housing space required will still be the same for each pig.

The facilities you use to raise and house your pig do not need to be elaborate or expensive structures. You may have sufficient space in an outbuilding that already exists on your property. Any building can be converted to living space or a portion of it divided into a suitable area.

One consideration would be to find a building that allows the pig access to an outdoor area. This is often with a door that can be closed in inclement weather or opened to allow spring and summer breezes to flow through.

There are three basic considerations for any structure being used for housing your pig: safety, convenience in cleaning out the bedding area, and comfort, which would include sufficient warmth or cooling in cold and hot weather, respectively. Depending on what is available on your property, you may need only a minimal alteration to adequately house your pig from a little animal to a large one.

Pigs are very smart animals and clean animals, contrary to most beliefs. Any designs for shelter or pens should take into account their behavior. A pig will typically assign a certain function to different areas of its living space. This is also true with multiple animals. If given a choice, they prefer a single sleeping area, which is generally the most comfortable area they can find; a separate area to deposit their manure (feces); and another area for eating and drinking.

If there is adequate room in the pen or other enclosure, most of the manure will be dropped

Raising pigs on pastures and open lots is the most humane method of growing pork. Freedom of movement is an essential ingredient for healthy pigs.

in areas away from where they sleep. You can also encourage this behavior by placing the water and feeding area near the opposite end from your pig's bedding area. Water spilled on the floor or dirt will be a cold place to lie, and unless the weather is hot, they will stay away from that area. You should also locate the feeding trough, tray, or pan a short distance away from the water supply and away from the sleeping area. Positioning a pen in such a manner will encourage your pig to quickly establish separate areas for eating and lying down, and this will help keep the area clean.

If there is a grassy area available near the building where you will keep your pig, you should strongly consider using it as a pasture area where your pig can get out of the building and roam around. Pigs love natural turf, and a grassy area will be a natural fit. One pig will utilize the available area. A large animal, one that is fully grown, will typically need about one-quarter acre, but less will suffice if you are limited in space. The important thing is to get the animal outside to encourage movement. This will have some effect on the muscle tone later when you butcher the animal, but mostly it is just good husbandry to allow an animal to roam outside. Pigs are curious and will investigate the same site hundreds of times during their life in the paddock.

The equipment you need to raise a pig does not have to be extensive. A small trough can be used for both feed and water.

different areas of your paddocks. They can move from site to site with your pig. Sturdy plastic or fiberglass huts, which are often used for dairy calves, are relatively inexpensive, easy to move because they are fairly lightweight, and can be found in many sizes and shapes. They typically have a window or other opening at the opposite end from the entrance, which allows airflow through it in hot weather. Because they are very versatile, these huts can be used for other animals or pets too.

Besides, an outdoor hut of some variety is a good investment if shade trees are not available. Pigs can tolerate cold weather better than hot, humid conditions. If they have shelter to get out of a bitter wind in winter, they can usually tolerate cold temperatures. This is not the case with heat.

Pigs do not sweat like humans. They tend to hold heat inside their bodies rather than it expiring through their skin. This is a useful physical quirk in winter but not so useful in hot summer conditions. Many people have an image of pigs being dirty because they lie in the mud. This is simply their reaction to hot weather. They are using the mud and moisture, which is often cooler than the ambient temperature, to cool their bodies. It may not be possible to dissuade your pig from rooting a space in the cool ground to lie in. It's their nature and you shouldn't be upset when it happens. Allow your pig to be itself and it will find its own best way to be comfortable.

You can construct an outdoor structure made of sturdy wood to house your pig. An A-frame design or a rectangular hut are easy to build and easily moved if you choose to place either in

Wood huts offer a good shelter from the hot sun and bitter cold weather. When straw or other bedding material is added, your pig will have a comfortable retreat.

They will need a shady place to retreat to in hot, sunny conditions. By having a hut of some sort, they can get out of the direct sunlight. Pigs can overheat quickly and may need attention, such as sprinkling their body with water, in extreme cases.

PIG BODIES

Like humans, pigs are monogastric, meaning they have a simple stomach, unlike cattle (ruminants that have more than one stomach compartment to aid digestion).

The body of a pig is more or less built around its digestive system. The stomach's main purpose is to break down complex proteins to feed muscle growth and maintenance. Proteins that are broken down are converted into amino acids. The large intestine absorbs the most water and is where most of the processing of feed takes place. The small intestine absorbs amino acids, fats, starches, sugars, and some water. After the majority of the feed has been processed, the remainder is converted into a bacterial mass called feces (manure), which is then expelled.

The kidneys are generally not thought of as part of the digestive system, although they filter waste materials from the bloodstream and send these wastes to the bladder to be excreted as urine. Approximately 60 percent of the manure is feces while 40 percent is urine.

It is important to understand these functions because these internal parts of the digestive system will be discussed later in the butchering process.

FENCING AND ENCLOSURES

Having satisfied the pig's housing needs, you should consider your fences and enclosures prior to bringing a pig on your property.

Fencing not only marks property lines, it also is an important part of humanely enclosing your animals, whether that's one pig or other livestock. Perimeter fences in particular are an important barrier between your property and your neighbor's.

If you own the property, you likely already know where your boundaries are. If you are considering purchasing a small-acreage farm, it is a good idea to investigate the property lines before signing any purchase agreement. Ask to walk and view the fence lines with the owner or real estate agent handling the sale to fully understand the boundaries. Missing fence rows may cause confusion as to the actual property line. Odd configurations may appear if fences have been trampled, moved, or torn out. Walking these lines can be instructive as you will notice many things about the condition of the fences, the property's terrain, and other things you might not readily perceive while riding in a vehicle or viewing the property from aerial maps.

There are two basic types of fences: permanent and temporary. Permanent fences are usually found along the perimeter and often define boundaries between farms. In earlier farming days, many farms had multiple permanent fences built within the perimeter fences as the variety of livestock, such as work horses, dairy cattle, beef cattle, and, yes, pigs, needed sturdier structures.

Permanent fences are constructed for long-term use and life, and sturdy materials are used. Temporary fences are intended for short-term use. They are usually found as enclosures within the boundary fences. They do not need to be as sturdily constructed because their intent is to be easily moved.

Pigs can be hard on fences for several reasons. Their rooting instinct drives them to poke their noses around their environment as they search for food or out of curiosity. The mechanics of their rooting around a paddock is best likened to shovel digging. They will begin to push with the tip of their snout (nose) and dig small holes or trenches as they pursue whatever has attracted their interest, perhaps tasty roots, interesting

Wire-panel fences are easy to construct for a paddock in which to raise your pig. They are easy to set up, and when done properly, they provide an escape-proof enclosure.

scents, or bugs and insects. This activity is normal and can lead them along fence lines where they may be able to lift the bottom part of the fence from the ground and create a possible escape route. Walk the fence line of any enclosure where you plan to put your pig and check for weaknesses in the line. Be sure to correct those you find or you may spend an afternoon retrieving your pig from outside your enclosure. One thing you will learn if this happens is that a pig will not likely find its escape hole when you try to return it to your pasture unless it is as big as a garage door. They are unlikely to return to the pasture through the same small opening they escaped. It is worth your time to thoroughly check your fencing prior to having any problems.

Normal pig behavior includes rooting around their paddock as they use their snout to dig up the soil. Good fences will keep them from using this practice to try to escape from their lot.

Young and small pigs typically are not a concern with fences until they grow to a larger size and begin to explore. A good reference for options of different enclosures and fences, and how to build them, can be found in *How to Raise Pigs*, available from Voyageur Press.

COSTS INVOLVED

Your startup costs may depend on several factors. We will focus solely on the cost of obtaining and raising your pig and exclude other things, such as buildings, equipment, and the farmland itself (if purchasing it).

Pigs for sale are categorized in several classes: feeder pigs, barrows and gilts, butcher hogs and sows (light and heavy), and boars.

Regardless of the breed you choose, your goal is to raise your piglet to a market weight in the shortest amount of time. Good growth is achieved with a sound diet appropriate to the pig's weight brackets. Start with a young pig because they are less expensive.

INITIAL STARTUP COSTS (APPROXIMATE)

Price for piglet	$50.00
Feed	$62.45
Shelter*	$350.00
Fencing**	$84.00
Bedding***	$18.00
Freezer	$250.00
Miscellaneous	$50.00
Total	$864.45

   * Shelter includes one fiberglass hut.
  ** Fencing includes 200 square feet to cover raising pig from 40 to 250 pounds if no pasture or out-lot is provided. This equals about a 16 × 16-foot lot made from wire panels. Each panel is 16 feet in length, requiring 4 panels at an approximate cost of $21.00 per panel.
*** Bedding includes six 55-pound bales of straw during winter months but one bale during summer months when pig has access to outside lot.

Let's assume you wish to purchase one single feeder pig to raise. A feeder pig is generally defined as a young pig that has been weaned from its mother and is now ready to be put on a full-feed diet. It no longer needs milk to grow and can transition to a dry, grain-based diet. Feeder pigs typically weigh between 25 and 40 pounds when sold at livestock markets or auctions. You may be able to purchase one pig or two from a local pig farmer who raises them in a traditional manner and at a lower weight. It is more difficult to purchase from large pig farms because of biosecurity concerns. Buying locally is your best choice if that option exists because that local farmer is trying his or her best to raise healthy, profitable pigs.

Feeder pigs at a livestock market or auction are generally sold in lots consisting of several dozens of pigs but auctioned off at an individual price, which is then multiplied by the number of pigs in that lot. It may not be possible to purchase a single pig out of such a lot unless you can discuss this with that lot's purchaser.

At the time of this writing, individual feeder pig prices range from $30 to $50 for a 40- to 50-pound pig. This price also depends on current market conditions and breed and pig availability. Purchasing a pig at the heavier weight often ensures that it is healthy and eating well, which will lead to a better growth rate for you. An unhealthy or unthrifty pig may be less expensive but generally doesn't grow as well as a healthy pig and will take longer and more feed to get it to reach a butchering weight. Buy a healthy pig even if it's more expensive that day and you will be happier with the results.

A barrow is a male pig that has been castrated, usually while still a feeder pig or soon after birth. They can be raised like any other pig, and there is the advantage of not having to work with a sexually intact male. Gilts are young female pigs that are considered older than feeder pigs but are not yet sexually mature. They can be raised like barrows and with barrows without having to contend with sexual activity in your pasture. Butcher hogs are those ready for market and may weigh from 180 pounds to 240 pounds. If you want to dive right into the butchering aspect without waiting for the growing period to finish, you may want to consider buying a butcher hog that is ready, well, for butchering.

Sows are mature females that have had a litter (young pigs) and generally will weigh more than 240 pounds. At markets they may exceed that weight and be sold when reaching 300 pounds or more, and they are then considered heavy sows. Boars are male pigs that can weigh from 180 to 400 pounds. These, however, will not be your best option for buying a pig to butcher due to the elevated testosterone levels when compared to barrows (castrated boars).

FEED COSTS

Feed costs will be the largest expense during the growing period between purchasing and butchering your pig.

Typically a pig will need between 3 to 4 pounds of feed per pound of weight gain. This is also referred to as rate of gain. The less feed needed to raise the pig to market weight, the less cost there is, resulting in a higher profit. This is why pig growers want highly efficient growing pigs, those that use less feed to grow to the optimum weight. This may not be as major a concern to you with one pig, but you also want it to grow well on less feed. Whatever your pig's efficiency rate, it will go through the three phases of production like any other feeder pig: nursery, growing, and finishing.

A simple crate is sufficient to transport a young pig to your farm, homestead, or small acreage. Be sure to check any local zoning ordinances relating to livestock production.

For example, let's say you purchase a 40-pound feeder pig and raise it to 210 pounds, a typical butchering weight. The 170 pounds of weight gain will require about 600 to 650 pounds of feed to reach that weight goal. These numbers can be multiplied times the cost of a grain mix that could be made up of corn, wheat, oats, soybeans or other protein sources, and minerals and vitamins. An example of the costs is given in the chart on page 230. Other plant byproducts, such as corn gluten meal, can be used to supplement expensive grains. One rule of thumb is that the energy level requirement is similar to all diets from the nursery stage to slaughter. However, the protein level changes as the pig grows.

One advantage of raising pigs is that they become porcine garbage disposals. Your household food waste may be fed to pigs, as well as garden excess. You will always find a willing audience for eating these waste products if you have pigs, so don't let them go to waste.

Regardless of the feeding program you develop, don't forget the water. Pigs need access to fresh water like any other animal, and you will need to make sure it is available at all times, even in freezing and cold winter weather.

COMPOSTING MANURE

A single pig will not produce a lot of manure, but you should explore an environmentally sound practice for handling whatever amount you end up with. But first, a few thoughts about manure.

The normal digestive process of a pig's gastrointestinal system produces feces like any other animal. Manure will quickly decompose under warm, moist soil conditions, and as it does, it releases chemical compounds such as nitrogen, phosphorus, potassium, and other nutrients into the soil. Field plants will absorb nutrients from the soil, so manure can be part of an important natural cycle.

Your single pig will not have the same impact as fifty, a hundred, or a thousand pigs. But that shouldn't mean you don't develop a way to handle its manure. After all, once your pig is in your freezer, you likely will clean up the area where it lived and maybe get it ready for the next animal.

So, how much manure does one pig produce in a day? Again, there is a range as the animal grows and increases its daily diet intake. The total amount of manure excreted by a pig is largely determined by the amount of feed it receives minus what the pig uses for muscle and bone growth and normal physical processes. This total increases as a pig grows from nursery to slaughtering weight. For example, from 50 to 120 pounds, one pig on a typical diet will produce about 6 pounds of manure each day. From 125 to 175 pounds, as its dietary intake increases even more, it will produce 8 pounds per day. And from 175 to 250 pounds, it will produce about 9½ pounds per day.

Let's say that your pig gains 1½ to 2 pounds of weight per day. This will require about 114 days (at a growth rate of 1¾ pounds per day, which is within a normal range) to achieve the 200 pounds of growth.

Then, 114 days times the average daily manure production of 8 pounds equals 920 pounds over the pig's lifetime, or time with you.

Part of this weight will be lost through evaporation of the water in manure. Plus, some is likely to be spread on your paddock, pasture, or fields while your pig is moving about, and which you will not collect.

So, what do you do with the manure you do have? Why not compost it? Composting is a process in which microorganisms convert organic materials, such as manure, bedding, leaves, and other plant materials, into soil-like matter. Simply piling manure and letting it sit is not really composting, however.

Young pigs can be raised in a very small area at first. They will soon outgrow their small enclosure quickly, and you will need to plan for a larger area for them.

Composting is an active process in which microbes and oxygen are the main catalysts for the transformation. The manure and bedding and any other organic matter is allowed to decay in a pile or windrow. As it decays, it creates heat that breaks down the organic compounds and neutralizes them.

The high nitrogen level in manure can burn plants when applied directly to your field or garden. In other words, composting will decay and convert organic matter from a volatile compound to a stable, neutralized fertilizer.

The full composting process won't happen overnight. To reach a neutralized state may take anywhere from 3 weeks to 8 months, depending on adequate oxygen and aeration of the pile, the temperature, the moisture content of the pile,

the correct mix of materials, and how closely it's managed.

Oxygen and aeration is needed for a good compost result. This involves either stirring or turning the pile mechanically or by hand-forking it so that air is introduced throughout the material. Perforated pipes can be used to blow air into the pile, but this often works best after the pile has been turned at least once.

Manure that is going through a composting cycle can create a lot of heat, and you want your pile to reach core temperatures of about 160°F. Compost thermometers are available to help monitor the internal temperature. This heat helps to break down volatile organic compounds (VOCs) and will help destroy weed seeds contained in the bedding or plants.

Moisture in a compost pile may be difficult to calculate, but it is needed to get a good result. A 40 to 60 percent moisture content is needed, about the same amount as a sponge that has been wrung out. If the moisture is too low, the material will likely mold rather than heat. If the moisture is too high, the compost pile won't allow enough heat to generate and will simply be a semisolid soggy mess. Interestingly, if you keep turning a too-high moisture content pile, enough of the moisture will eventually evaporate and reach the right proportion of mix where it will activate the compost's heating process. How closely you manage your pile will have an effect on your success with it.

Lastly, a successful compost pile will consist of the right mix of materials, or the carbon (C) to nitrogen (N) ratio. An ideal ratio of C:N would fall in the range of 25:1 to 30:1, but you can achieve good results with a range of 20:1 to 40:1.

This ratio will be influenced by the amount of wood bedding materials, such as sawdust or shavings, in the mix. Too much will result in a high C:N ratio. Some nitrogen sources, such as grass clippings, additional raw manure, or even nitrogen fertilizer, added to the mix may be needed to balance this ratio. Using chopped straw for your bedding materials can help to keep this ratio lower.

Composting serves several other purposes besides transforming manure into a stable nutrient form for your garden:

- It reduces the volume you need to dispose of or spread on your field, paddocks, or garden.

- It will add organic matter to wherever you use it.

- It will reduce the presence of flies by eliminating their breeding ground.

- It will reduce any parasite reinfestation since the heat will kill parasite eggs.

- It neutralizes ammonia gases and certain pathogens such as E. coli.

- It kills weed seeds, as they cannot survive the heating process.

Many compost designs are available and you should look for one that suits your situation. These may include stacking the manure in confined piles, storing in compost bins, and air-piping. A variety of composting methods are explained in *The Family Cow Handbook: A Guide to Keeping a Milk Cow* or *The Complete Illustrated Guide to Farming*, both available from Voyageur Press. Turn your pig's manure into a resource rather than looking at it as a liability.

FEEDING YOUR PIG

A healthy pig will grow fast. The small pig you start with will quickly become a large animal to be butchered about 4 months later.

A grain-based diet is typical for fast-growing pigs. Along with household scraps, pigs can consume a variety of feedstuffs in their rations.

TYPICAL ENERGY SOURCES FOR PIGS

Grain	Feed Value	Maximum Ration Content for Sow and Pigs
Corn	100%	100%
Wheat	95%	50–75%
Milo	95%	50–75%
Barley	90%	25–50%
Oats	80%	25–50%

it takes more feed (added costs) to increase the total weight of the pig because more nutrients are needed to maintain a larger body form than for a smaller body. This also means the optimum cost ratio of pounds of feed for a pound of gain will likely fall in the 200- to 240-pound range. Anything over this will cost more to increase the pig's weight. Certainly a home-raised pig can be butchered at 180 to 190 pounds and still supply a lot of meat for your family. You may want to calculate several different weight-to-cost ratios to find one best to your liking.

While pigs can grow on a variety of feedstuffs, including pastures, their main source of protein and starches for growth are grains such as corn and soybeans. These high carbohydrate and protein plants will help develop good growth rates that will enable you to have them reach a butchering weight in the shortest time. Plus, a high-quality diet will make the meat taste better later on when you cook it.

The protein levels required for growth provided by the feed ration don't vary greatly from a 50-pound feeder pig to a 250-pound finished hog. It is roughly 13 to 16 percent. The quantity of feed varies more than the protein percentage.

Cereal grains, such as wheat, barley, milo, and oats, can help meet the protein requirements but are often too low in protein to be used alone. They may be mixed with other protein sources from oilseed meals, such as soybean meal or canola meal. Animal byproducts, such as fish meal, bone meal, dried skim milk, and whey products, may also be used as high-quality protein sources. But these are generally more expensive and may have limited availability.

Generally speaking, the law of diminishing returns kicks in as the pig grows larger. This means

PROTEIN LEVELS REQUIRED BY SWINE

Ration	Protein %
Creep Feeding	18–20%
Growing (50–125 lbs.)	15–16%
Finishing (125–250 lbs.)	13–14%
Young gilts & boars	15–16%
Older sows & boars	13–14%

APPROXIMATE WATER AND FEED CONSUMPTION

Pig Weight (lbs.)	# Dry Feed/ day	# Water/ day	Gallons/ day/ approx.
50	4	8–12	1–1.5
100	6	12–18	1.5–2.2
150	8	16–24	2.0–3.0
200	10	20–30	2.5–3.5
250	12	24–36	3.0–3.5

MIXED RATIONS

(Based on a 1-ton mix, with approximate costs based on July 2015 market prices)

Baby Pig: 20%		Young Pig: 18% (10–50 lbs.)	
1000# Yellow Corn	$0.08/lb. = $80.00	1000# Yellow Corn	$0.08/lb. = $80.00
200# Rolled Oats	$0.09/lb. = $18.00	200 # Rolled Oats	$0.09/lb. = $18.00
250# Dried Whey	$0.15/lb. = $40.00	250 # Dried Whey	$0.15/lb. = $40.00
500# Soybean Meal	$0.20/lb. = $100.00	500# Soybean Meal	$0.20/lb. = $100.00
50# Vitamin-Minerals	$0.40/lb. = $20.00	50# Vitamin-Minerals	$0.40/lb. = $20.00
	$258/ton = $0.13/lb.		$258/ton = $0.13/lb.
Growing Pig: 16% (50–125 lbs.)		**Finishing Pig: 14% (125–250 lbs.)**	
1550# Yellow Corn	$0.08/lb.= $124.00	1600# Yellow Corn	$0.08/lb. = $128.00
400# Soybean Meal	$0.20/lb. = $36.00	350# Soybean Meal	$0.20/lb. = $70.00
50# Vitamin-Minerals	$0.40/lb. = $20.00	50# Vitamin-Minerals	$0.40/lb. = $20.00
	$180/ton = $0.11/lb.		$218/ton = $0.09/lb.

OTHER NUTRIENT SOURCES

It is not protein specifically that pigs need, but rather amino acids for the formation of muscles and other body functions. Twenty amino acids are needed for proper pig growth with ten required as dietary essentials. Other grain and plant byproducts that can be substituted into the diet include corn gluten meal, hominy feed, brewer's products, distiller's grain, wheat bran, and alfalfa meal.

Small quantities of minerals and vitamins are required for many metabolic processes in pigs. These are important because they aid in the development of strong bones and teeth and are required for proper muscle contraction, hormone function, and blood clotting. The growth and health of your pig can be severely affected by failing to provide sufficient amounts of minerals and vitamins.

More than fifteen minerals have been identified as essential for pig growth. Calcium, phosphorus, and iodized salt combine for the largest requirements. Other important minerals, such as iron, copper, zinc, and manganese, can be supplied in a trace-mineralized salt combination. Premixes with vitamins and minerals can be purchased as supplements, but they can be very expensive. Fortunately, the most needed minerals and vitamins are readily available, can be easily mixed into their feed, and are relatively inexpensive.

HOW MUCH DOES A PIG EAT?

As stated earlier, your pig will require more feed as it grows older. This increase allows for muscle and bone development as the body increases in size, and it requires more energy and protein for physical maintenance. For example, small pigs convert feed into body weight very efficiently. As a pig grows, it takes more feed per pound of weight gain. Overall, however, an approximate average of 3 pounds of feed will be required per pound of gain throughout a pig's life. The average amount of feed required daily can be examined in the accompanying chart.

The feed requirements generally conform into three divisions, which typically correspond with different weight ranges: young pig (10 to 50 pounds), growing pig (50 to 125 pounds), and finishing pig (125 to 250 pounds).

From the accompanying chart, we can assume your pig will require approximately 625 pounds of feed from 10 pounds to 250 pounds, not including any pasture, which can supplement grains and lower the total grain intake and cost. These are only approximate figures and yours may vary greatly depending on a number of factors, including grain prices in your area and your use of lower-cost feed supplements, or substitutes such as your family's food refuse. But it will give you a general idea of how to calculate your costs and how much it will cost to feed your pig from beginning to end. If you raise two pigs, then your costs will likely double. But, again, you can sell one to a livestock market and use that income to cover its feed cost.

From these feed cost calculations, we can also make some approximate projections as to your startup costs and investment, and use that to determine what your cost per pound of processed meat will be. In other words, what will it cost you to produce the meat you will be butchering and how does that cost compare to what you can buy in a local meat market without all the effort of raising a piglet to pork on your table?

Let's assume (without addition of pasture to supplement grains):

10 to 50 pounds requires 1.5 pounds of feed per pound of gain,

then, 40 pounds of gain $\times$ 1.5 pounds of feed = 60 pounds feed

---

50 to 125 pounds requires 2.5 pounds of feed per pound of gain,

then, 75 pounds of gain $\times$ 2.5 = about 190 pounds feed

---

125 to 250 pounds requires 3 pounds of feed per pound of gain,

then, 125 pounds of gain $\times$ 3 = 375 pounds feed

total feed required for 240 pounds of gain	625 pounds

---

then,

10 to 50 pounds = \$0.13/lb. (feed cost per pound)	= \$7.80
50 to 125 pounds = \$0.11/lb.	= \$20.90
125 to 250 pounds= \$0.09/lb.	= \$33.75
Total feed cost	\$62.45

The chart on page 17 lists some of the initial costs involved when starting out new. These are approximate costs and don't include processing fees if you choose to have your pig butchered by a local meat market, fuel costs for transport, and other incidental costs such as electricity, investment of your land, and so on. But, again, we can show some costs that will give you a clearer idea of how to determine those associated with your pig.

Using the sample startup costs and feed costs, we can apply them to get an overall cost to raise your pig. Then we can estimate the amount of meat you will harvest from your pig and calculate the cost per pound to get it to your freezer or table. Again, these are approximate costs involved and yours may differ in the end. One thing to remember with the startup costs is that generally their greatest expense is at the start. Once you have the fences built, the shelter set, the freezer in place for the meat, and some of the miscellaneous costs paid for in the first year, the cost of producing the next pig drops dramatically because you have mainly the feed and purchase costs to consider. The chart on page 35 will give you some idea of this dynamic.

FORAGES AND PASTURES

The use of pastures and forages to form part of your pig's diet has received much attention in recent years. Although this was a traditional way used to raise pigs, it was replaced by many confinement systems that improved the rates of gain but took pigs from outside and put them indoors.

As pork producers today are developing niche markets for their pork products, their pigs are once again allowed to roam in pastures and consume forages as part of their diet. Even though a pig's monogastric digestive system does not lend itself to using great quantities of forages, pastures can provide your pig with quality protein and certain vitamins, and can help reduce the total feed requirement from supplements and grains. This can help lower the total feeding cost of raising your pig to a finished weight. Pork producers who use pastures to supplement their pig's diets also extol the outdoor aspect of this production system and that it is more natural for a pig than being totally raised indoors.

Generally these savings can amount to 3 to 10 percent of the grain and about as much as half of the protein needed for growing and finishing pigs. That is a significant savings. Other factors such as the type of pasture, the age of the pigs, and your overall management system will also have an effect. The biggest savings include lower feed costs from less purchased grains. Also, manure production will be distributed around the pasture or field rather than being deposited in or near the stable.

Regardless of whether you use pastures extensively or minimally in your feeding program, your pig will benefit from the exercise that will help develop muscle mass and muscle tone, being out in the sunlight that will help produce a better-quality fat for rendering because of adequate vitamin D levels, and will be more comfortable moving around than being sedentary in a confined space. This will also be a more humane way of raising your pig and should provide many satisfactory hours for you and your family of watching it out in a natural setting.

Ration formulation is possible with many computer programs available today. Also, most animal feed companies or supply outlets can help you develop a ration that fits your situation and budget. County agricultural extension agents have access to ration formulation programs that may be helpful to you, and they can offer advice of where to seek additional help.

HEALTHY PIG MEANS HEALTHY MEAT

You will use your husbandry skills to provide your pig with a safe, comfortable, and fulfilling existence. As a pig owner, you have the ethical responsibility to provide your animal with conditions in which it can grow from quality feeds, reside without fear, and be treated in a gentle and humane manner. In many ways, the more you work with your pig, the more the pig may become an extension of your family. This may seem unusual, but it is in your best interests, financially and philosophically, to have a pig that is content and easy to work with.

HEALTH CONCERNS

Any pork producer knows that pigs can get sick even with the best of care. The key is to minimize the severity of any illness to the greatest extent possible. This starts with observing your pig every day. You will learn quickly to observe its normal movements and routine, and distinguish them from anything that appears abnormal.

Your observations can be made in the morning or evening during feeding times, or during the day. Quickly identifying listlessness or behavior that doesn't seem normal, such as not eating, can limit any potential damage. A pig that exhibits symptoms of illness will generally need some intervention from you or a licensed veterinarian, who can dispense certain antibiotics if needed.

You will become your pig's diagnostician and perhaps its pharmacist or doctor. Depending on your program, philosophies, and goals, three treatment systems can be used with your pig: conventional, homeopathic, and herbal. Each has advantages and disadvantages, and you should study them thoroughly to decide which may align best with you and your situation. *How to Raise Pigs* is a book that can explain much of this for you.

If you use conventional treatments involving antibiotics—and in some cases this may be the best choice to save your pig's life—be aware that there are specific withdrawal times after an injection or oral antibiotics have been administered. There will be a period of time during which it is illegal to sell an animal over the market or to be used for human consumption. This time will eventually end as the animal's system filters out any antibiotic residue and the meat will be safe for you to eat. These precautions and times are clearly stated or labeled on bottles or packages containing antibiotics.

Also, if you administer medications by injection, you need to be careful where you insert the needle. If intermuscular injections need to be given—those where the needle is inserted into a muscle—it should be done in the neck muscles. Avoid placing injections into the hams, loin areas, and shoulders because any residual puncture marks in the muscle will remain when the carcass is cut up.

PIG BEHAVIOR

What can you expect from your live pig, especially if you've never raised one? First, pigs respond to the treatment they receive. Pigs that are comfortable around people have had positive interaction with humans. Negative experiences resulting from mistreatment, handling, or neglect generally result in a large flight zone. This is the sensory bubble surrounding an animal where you can only get so close to the pig before it moves away. Positive experiences between pig and human will shrink this zone and allow you to touch, rub, scratch, brush, or easily handle them. Negative experiences will widen this zone so that you cannot get very close to them.

Pigs are gregarious by nature and can be quite social. This is one reason you should consider raising two pigs at the same time rather than one. If you only raise one pig, it is wise to place

Pigs are very social animals and respond to the treatment they receive. They can become very comfortable around humans and will interact with people if unafraid of them.

it where it may see, hear, or even interact with other farm animals. Again, you can consider selling the other animal to market after you've chosen which one you will butcher. Pigs have a history of being mortgage lifters, and this income may offset the cost of raising both of them. Pigs can be curious, gentle, and display an almost humanlike affection if handled in a proper and humane manner.

PIG BREEDS

Is there a best kind of pig or breed to raise? Does one breed have better-tasting meat than another? Many who raise pigs to butcher have asked these questions. The emergence of interest in artisan foods has also encouraged producers to supply these markets with animals from less common breeds because of their unique meat qualities.

The economic dynamics of the pork industry between the 1960s and 1980s saw the commercialization of certain swine breeds that adapted easily to mass production systems to the point where only eight major breeds remain today: Landrace, Berkshire, Chester White, Duroc, Hampshire, Poland China, Spotted Poland China, and Yorkshire.

However, minor swine breeds that teetered toward extinction have now been brought back as heritage or heirloom breeds. These include the Hereford, Large Black, Mulefoot, Red Wattle, and Tamworth.

The Berkshire breed has a good growth rate and yields an exceptional flavor in its meat.

As these heritage breeds have become recognized again for their unique meat qualities because of their genetics, they are finding favor with chefs, homesteaders, and others who appreciate their distinctive separation from the mainstream breeds.

Landrace—a white hog noted for its long body and having sixteen or seventeen pairs of ribs, which translates into more cuts of meat per animal.

Berkshire—a black hog with white lower legs. It is noted for good growth rates and the exceptional flavor of its meat, which is darker, has a higher pH, and contains more intramuscular fat or marbling.

Chester White—are popular among pork producers because they are good mothers that produce large litters and are typically sound, durable animals.

Duroc—have a hair color that can range from a light golden, bordering on yellow, to a dark red, similar to mahogany. It has drooping ears and is appreciated for its feed efficiency.

Hampshire—one of the most recognizable breeds with its black markings and distinctive white belt over the shoulders and down the front legs. They produce a lean carcass with good muscle quality.

Poland China—is noted as a big-framed, long-bodied, lean and muscular breed. They lead the United States in pork production and are known for their black color, with six white points: the feet, tail, and tip of the nose.

Spotted Poland China—have floppy ears and black spots of varying sizes across both sides of the body. They have excellent meat qualities and are known for their good feed efficiency. The females are known to be docile and easy to handle.

Yorkshire—grow fast and have good feed conversion rates. Also have long bodies and produce an excellent carcass.

Hereford—a heritage breed with a pattern of intense red and white trim around the edges of its body. They are quiet and docile and very adaptable to a variety of climates. They perform well on pastures and produce an excellent carcass.

Large Black—a distinctive heritage breed that produces a lean pork and bacon that is tender and fine textured. Though fewer in number than other breeds, Large Black pigs have a loyal following by those who raise them.

Mulefoot—is distinctive because of its solid, noncloven hoof. Their dark, moist meat is excellent for hams, lard, and home curing. They also fatten well on many kinds of forage.

Red Wattle—a large, red hog with a distinctive flesh wattle attached to each side of its head. They are hardy, grow rapidly, and have great foraging abilities. They can adapt to a wide range of climates.

Tamworth—have a red, almost ginger color to their hair coat. They are adaptable to many different climates and are tolerant of extreme changes in temperature. Their meat is lean and they work well in pasture-grazing systems.

The genetics of a specific breed will influence many of the meat and muscle qualities, but a pig is still reliant on the feed it receives to impart a distinct flavor. Just think of the acorn-fed pigs of Italy or the truffle-influenced meat flavor of France, and you will get a sense of this exceptional difference. The point is that you can try to influence the flavor of your pig's meat by what you feed it, but it still mostly comes down to its genetic inheritance. However, if you have acorns available, use it in the feed ration. While you likely don't have truffles, you may be growing something else that could lightly hint at a different flavor.

How to Raise Pigs provides an in-depth look at each of the breeds mentioned here. Securing a heritage breed pig to raise may be more expensive initially and perhaps more difficult to locate for purchase, but your rewards will come from a flavor you've never before experienced.

You now have learned what you need to do to get started. Now go out and find your pig!

The Large Black is one of several heritage breeds you can raise. Although their population is small in total numbers, their popularity is increasing because they produce a lean pork and tasty bacon.

Chapter 2
BUTCHERING AT HOME

So now you have raised your pig to the weight you want. The next step is to get it into your freezer or on your plate.

Generations of farm families have home-butchered pigs as a way to store meat over long periods. Processing a live animal into edible portions was not only a family-oriented event, but could include a wide circle of friends and relatives as a social gathering.

The butchering of farm animals—whether beef, pork, sheep, or chickens—was traditionally a late-year activity because of the cooler temperatures, especially before the advent of electric refrigeration. It was risky to butcher on warm summer days because high temperatures could quickly ruin the meat or decrease its quality. Cooler days made the strenuous work a little easier and gave the workers a little more time as the fresh meat would not spoil as quickly.

Although refrigeration is prevalent today, especially in meat markets that slaughter animals, you may not have access to it if you butcher at home. This does not mean you can't process a carcass at home; it only means you need to be aware of ambient temperatures when you butcher an animal.

This chapter will look at all the issues involved with and the steps to be taken in harvesting a live animal and safely working with the resulting carcass.

FIRST STEPS

Home butchering is not for the faint of heart, but it also is a process that you and your family, along with help from friends, can complete with some guidance. The whole process and sequence of steps involved to safely and humanely kill a pig—which in simple terms is what you will be doing—and end up with packaged meat in your freezer will take some physical stamina. The full range of the butchering experience includes killing your pig, quickly deconstructing the carcass, packaging it, and freezing it. Once the process begins, you will need to carry through to the end or you will have spoiled meat.

There will be noises and odors that you may not have experienced before. However, this should not deter you from doing it and doesn't mean you can't become very good at it. Simply remember that it won't be the same experience you have walking up to a meat case at the local market and selecting your favorite pork cuts. You will get them from your pig, but it will be through your efforts.

Home butchering will appeal to those who value self-sufficiency, are adept at or have some knife skills, have the necessary equipment, and can process a carcass in a short time window so that the meat doesn't spoil.

You have three options when the pig you've raised has reached the desired weight and you are ready to butcher it: doing it yourself, locating a local licensed meat business to kill and dress the carcass for you, or a combination of these two.

Because one of the main points of this book is to explain the home butchering process, we will focus on that. You can contact a local meat market that slaughters and processes pigs and arrange to deliver your pig there and let them kill the pig, dress the carcass by removing the internal organs, and then cool it before you retrieve the carcass. This will allow you to work with a chilled carcass several days later to cut up

at your home. You may have several advantages with this option.

First, it takes the killing process out of your hands if you don't feel you can successfully accomplish it. And there's no shame in acknowledging this. In fact, it may be a safer and more humane route than for you to attempt to restrain a live animal and then kill it. Botched attempts at killing a live animal usually have adverse outcomes for both the animal and the person doing it.

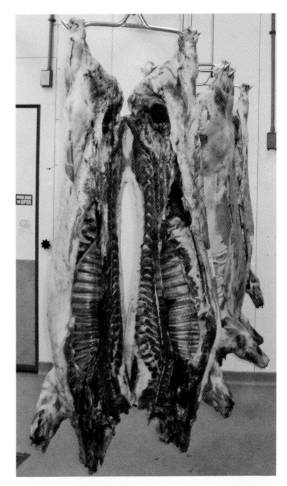

Envision the two halves of a pig's carcass during your preparation time before butchering. This will be a large amount of meat to process in a short time.

A variety of knives can be used to cut up a carcass. A metal meat saw will be needed to cut through hard bones. From left to right: 6-inch sticking knife, 10-inch breaking knife, 8-inch breaking knife, 4-inch boning knife, 4-inch skinning knife, cavity spreader, bone scraper, and 6-inch straight knife.

Secondly, arranging to retrieve the two halves of a chilled, split carcass at different times will allow you to cut up one half at a time. This will lighten your load of having to quickly deal with both halves at the same time, if that can be arranged.

If you choose this path, you will need to be ready to process the half carcass once you get it home, unless you have a large chest freezer in which to temporarily store it. You can cut the carcass into smaller units to make it fit so you can work on one section at a time. This option also gives you more time to cut up a carcass than would be available with a just-dispatched pig that is lying on a floor and needs to be quickly processed.

INITIAL PREPARATION

You need to develop a plan of all the steps involved before, during, and after the butchering. You don't want to go blindly into this important part without knowing where you are heading.

Having a plan will minimize mistakes, reduce the chance of injury to yourself or anyone helping you, and keep the meat from spoiling.

Set a target date for butchering and arrange your schedule to fit around it. Begin planning your steps as much as a week in advance. This will allow you time to

- arrange for help because you likely will not be able to kill a pig on your own

- acquire or assemble the necessary equipment to restrain the pig and then lift it once it's been killed

- secure the appropriate knives and meat saws needed to deconstruct the carcass

- reduce any surprises during the butchering process

The first time you home butcher will be the hardest because all the steps will be new and you may feel awkward with it. But once you've accomplished it, you may find you have a new talent.

LET'S TALK NUMBERS

How much meat will you have to store? You need to plan for a large quantity of meat for your freezer from cutting up the carcass. Close estimates can be made for calculating a market weight, a dressing or hanging weight, and finally into the weight of various cuts. First, some definitions will provide a common language used in understanding the meat industry.

Market weight carries two meanings depending on the intent. It can refer to the target weight you are trying to achieve with your pig, say, 200 to 240 pounds. It can also mean the weight at the time a pig is sent to market, which may have a range between 225 to 250 pounds, or higher.

Hanging weight, dressed weight, or "on the rail" are terms used interchangeably to refer to the pounds of the carcass after the pig has been killed and eviscerated. At this stage the carcass has been split down the spine into two halves and the head has been removed. This is the weight for which local butchers will charge you if the pig is taken to them for processing, plus any additional fees involved with killing the pig.

Several other terms are helpful to understand, including side, dressing percentage, shrinkage, and cutting yield. You may encounter these terms being tossed around by local butchers, and knowing what they mean will make it less confusing. They all reference a carcass in various phases after the kill has been made.

- A side refers to one-half of the entire carcass. The carcass is split down the spine to help it cool better and to make the total weight of the carcass more manageable to cut up. Lifting half a carcass is easier than

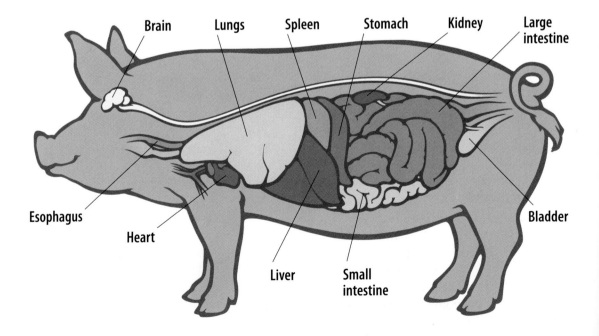

a whole one. A side of pork includes one matched forequarter and hindquarter of the same side.

- Dressing percentage is the proportion of the live weight that remains intact in the carcass after kill and before deconstruction. It is sometimes referred to as the yield. It is calculated as carcass weight ÷ live weight × 100 = dressing percentage

- Shrinkage is the weight loss that may occur throughout the processing sequence. It may happen due to moisture or tissue loss from both the fresh and processed product.

- Cutting yield is the proportion of the weight that is a useable or saleable product after trimming and subdivision of the whole carcass.

We can do some calculations to help you estimate how much meat there will be to work with. While these numbers may not exactly apply to your pig, the formula used will apply regardless of how much your pig actually weighs. And, you can do these estimates even before you begin to raise your pig, or while it is still small.

Let's say you have a pig that has reached a live weight of 240 pounds. Let's also say that you expect a dressing weight of 75 percent, which is within a normal range.

The total carcass weight then would equal 180 pounds (240 × .075 = 180). This means there will be 90 pounds per side (180 ÷ 2 = 90). At this point, this total will include the meat, bones, and fat, but not much of the blood as most of it would have been drained from the carcass during the early hanging period.

We can use an average cutout weight (cutting yield) for pigs that is about 60 percent. This equals 108 pounds (180 × 0.60 = 108). The other 72 pounds represent parts that typically aren't used, including fat trim, bones, and skin (although you will find uses for them as this book explains).

The 108 pounds of yield can be further broken down into sections. The largest parts of the pig carcass are the hams, which can each be about 23 percent of the dressed weight. In our example, this equals about 25 pounds (108 × 0.23 = 24.8).

The side or belly and the loin areas each represent about 15 percent of the carcass, or 32 pounds total (108 × 0.15 = 16.2 each or 32.4 for both).

The picnic and Boston butt are each about 10 percent of the carcass, or 21 pounds (108 × 0.10 = 10.8, times 2 = 21.6 pounds, more or less).

COST OF MEAT

For first year:

210-pound live pig = 150-pound carcass = 120 pounds of eating meat

120 pounds of meat ÷ $864.45 = $7.20 per pound

For second year:

210-pound live pig = 150 pound carcass = 120 pounds of eating meat

120 pounds of meat ÷ 136.00* = $1.13 per pound

* The second year will include purchase price, feed, and bedding costs. It will not include shelter, fencing, freezer, or miscellaneous costs, although these may be amortized.

CARCASS YIELD

(Assuming a 210-pound pig yielding a 150-pound carcass.)

	Approximate % of Dressed Weight	Approximate Pounds
1-Ham	18%	27
2-Pork Loin Chops and Roasts	16%	24
3-Bacon	16%	24
4-Spareribs	4%	6
5-Boston Butts	6%	10
6-Picnic Shoulders	7%	9
7-Pork Hocks	3%	4
8-Head	5%	8
9-Feet	3%	5
10-Lard	16%	24
Internal organs, waste	6%	9

There will be miscellaneous portions, including the jowl, feet, neck bones, skin, fat, bone and shrink, that will typically account for about 25 percent of the entire carcass weight, or about 27 pounds.

There may be some variance between pigs, but these percentages generally hold true for normal, well-developed pigs of that weight range.

THE PROCESS

So, after much thought, you've decided to plunge ahead and butcher your live pig at home. It will be an experience you won't soon forget and a story you can regale your friends with later. What is there to know, right? You kill the pig and go from there.

Before heading down this path, three words need to be seared into your mind: safety, safety, safety. For you and those who work with you, and for the pig.

"Why the pig?" you might ask. Since you are going to kill it anyway, why should its safety be an issue?

A sturdy table is essential to hold the weight of the carcass while you work with it. Always make certain the surface is clean and maintain cleanliness through the whole process.

Well, mainly because your pig is not likely to enjoy this experience. And too many distasteful and dangerous things can happen in a chaotic situation when guns, knives, and frightened animals are involved in close proximity.

Let's start first with your plan. You should make a list of all the steps needed to maneuver your pig to a convenient spot to kill it. You should make a list of all the necessary equipment and butchering tools needed to handle the pig and resulting carcass. These lists should be made well in advance, say several weeks, of when you set the butchering date. You should review diagrams of the skeletal structure, the digestive system, and placement of the internal organs, and you should have an understanding of the circulatory system so that you can make a clean, swift cut to the jugular vein for bleeding.

You will need to pay attention to cleanliness at all times once you start eviscerating the carcass. You need to be careful not to contaminate the carcass or organs with dirt, dust, flies, insects, and any other foreign matter. This requires that you find a level space, preferably a cement garage floor where you can have the greatest control over these conditions. Depending on the time of year you plan to butcher, heavy-duty, portable fans will help keep the air moving and deter flies, bugs, and insects from wanting to participate in this process. It is best if you do not include pets in your activity, especially in the run-up time to dispatching your pig so that it does not become agitated more than necessary.

LOCATION

It is best to use a shed or garage with a cement floor. This will keep dust to a minimum. Sweep the floor clean and wash it with disinfectant if you have the chance. Being under cover will provide a better atmosphere in case of inclement weather. No one likes to cut up meat in the rain or snow.

Several days before butchering, you will want to build a pen in your building to keep your pig. Moving it into this pen will help acclimate it to the new surroundings and you can put down bedding, feed, and water there. This will reduce the stress for the pig and likely for yourself and

Close confinement prior to butchering is essential to maintaining a calm pig. Make sure the floor and surrounding area is clean and free of obstacles.

your helpers since it will minimize the distance the carcass has to be moved.

If you plan to scald the pig to remove the hair and make use of the skin, you can set up a scalding tub outside where it can be filled and the water heated before beginning. You will need a reliable and convenient heating arrangement for your vat and a means of swinging the carcass with a block and tackle, or some other lifting method, such as a skid-steer loader or tractor with a front-end loader, to safely place the carcass into the boiling water. Pig carcasses can be hung from tree limbs if strong enough or from heavy gambrel sticks.

Whichever method you use will require enough strength and support to hold a large pig upside down without collapsing and still be near enough to the scalding vat and cooling tub.

Collect a proper set of butchering tools for using during the day. These should include a sticking knife, a skinning knife, a boning knife, a butcher knife, a sharpening steel, a cleaver, a meat saw, and meat hooks. Other items that will be used are thermometers, hair scrapers if scalding and taking off the hair, hand wash buckets, dry towels, soap, and clean catch buckets or tubs.

PREPPING YOUR PIG

Use a small, solitary pen to house your pig several days before the planned event. You can restrict the amount of feed each day with decreasing amounts. This will decrease the amount of material in its stomach and intestines while still keeping its nutrition stable.

Give it plenty of water up until about six hours before the planned butchering. Then restrict its availability. Like with humans, this will keep the pig hydrated, which is an important component in helping regulate its muscle temperature. You cannot control the weather's ambient temperature, so if the day ends up being hot or humid, provide a fan and keep the pig as cool as possible. You may have to provide water in this case so that the pig doesn't overheat. Your goal is to do whatever is needed to provide a cool and calm environment to keep your pig rested and quiet. If its body temperature rises above normal levels, the resulting meat can easily become feverish. If that happens, it will be more difficult to chill it properly, and poorly chilled meat cannot be properly cured. Never butcher a pig that is overheated, excited, or fatigued because this will prompt a condition known as souring, which is affected by temperature and an adrenaline release into its system.

BACTERIA CONCERNS

Natural forms of bacteria are found in the blood and tissues of a live pig, and other livestock as well. Until recently, it was thought that all muscle tissue was, basically, sterile if it had not been injured, cut into, or bruised. However, researchers have now found viable bacteria within muscle tissue of animals that appear normal and healthy. If your pig has had cuts or bruises to its body, you will need to look closely at those spots when cutting up the carcass, and perhaps remove any damaged meat tissue and discard it.

Any bacteria that exists within a live pig's muscles must be prevented from multiplying until the meat can be cured. This is also one reason butchering was historically done in the early spring and late fall before the advent of electrical refrigeration—it was cool or cold. You should think of it as a race between the bacterial action in the blood and tissue that are waiting to multiply when given the opportunity and the processes you use to inhibit that growth. It is a race you need to win to have safe food to eat or not have it spoil.

ABOUT SCALDING AND HAIR REMOVAL

This book is written to provide accurate information of all processes you can use to butcher your pig and harvest the meat. It includes precautions to take; it tries to alert you to avoid difficult or harmful situations that may unexpectedly and suddenly arise. However, it won't try to dissuade you from trying or experiencing a variety of activities.

There is one major cautionary notice, however, that is given for scalding the pig's carcass and scraping off the hair. We will go into a discussion later in this book about how to use the skin for making different crispy treats if you have the desire to utilize all the pig's parts. To use the skin, you will need to remove the hair, and this can be done in two ways: razor removal and scalding. Unless you have a great need for the bristly hair or even the skin, then this scalding step can be eliminated and the skin completely removed with the hair still intact. This pelt can then be discarded or composted.

Scalding a pig carcass, while it's entirely possible to do a good, safe job of it, is a laborious and dangerous process. You are working with extremely hot water in a large vat into which you need to submerge the entire heavy weight of the dead pig. This will require the killing be done in close proximity to the hot water and having a sturdy method of lifting and transporting that carcass to the vat and then being able to slowly submerge it into the hot water without splashing on anyone and causing severe burns. And then to remove this hot carcass, you will need to lay it on a table and let people scrape off the hair quickly so that you can open the carcass.

If you can safely manage all this with confidence, then go ahead. However, you will need to evaluate the value of the skin against the time lost in cutting up the carcass, plus the safety factor for yourself and anyone helping you. If you can't assure their or your complete safety, then perhaps it is not worth the risk to remove the hair and skin by this method. Severe burns are simply not worth the risk for some pigskin. If you have a local butcher do the killing and chilling, the butcher will remove the hair and the skin will still be intact for you to trim and use later.

Scalding

OK, so you have decided to scald the carcass. First, the tank or vat you use for boiling water to make scalding possible needs to be large enough to immerse the pig completely. Few metal barrels are constructed in a way to completely submerge the pig while still being able to watch and monitor the process. It takes a long time to heat up that much water to get it to boiling, so if you use this process, you will need to start heating the water long before you dispatch the pig. Also, you will need to track the time the carcass spends in the boiling water to keep it from cooking the muscles. There will be a temperature difference between the boiling water and the carcass, and once the carcass is immersed in the vat, the water will need to reheat to reach boiling.

Gas or propane heaters will work best because they can provide a steady flame that can be quickly increased in volume. Using a pit fire with wood will take much longer to heat the water and will need attention as the flames die down. It will be more difficult to maintain the appropriate temperature with a wood fire, plus you will have the added safety concerns of an open flame.

For proper scalding, you will need to keep the water temperature between 150 and 160°F. Once the water starts to boil, you can back the temperature down to that level. It is easier to come down with the temperature than get it to rise to the degrees you need. You will need a good thermometer to monitor the temperature at all times.

If you use a long horizontal tank, you should rotate the carcass until the hair starts to rub off, which may take 2 or 3 minutes. If using a smaller barrel tank, first lower the carcass head first into the water and submerge it as far as possible. Then lift it out and place the hooks in the lower jaw and lower the rear end into the water.

Be aware that this is a difficult process under the best of circumstances at home, but not necessarily impossible to accomplish. Be sure that all hooks are securely in place because you do not want the carcass to slip off. Retrieving a loose, heavy carcass in hot water will be difficult, and the longer it stays in the water the more the muscles will heat and cook.

Scraping

After removing the carcass from the hot water, you can lay it on a heavy table and begin to scrape off the hair. Using a hair scraper, or the blades of a dull knife, start first at the head and feet as these areas cool quickest. Your scraping strokes should go in the direction the hair lays, as it will come off easier. After finishing with the hair, use your scraper or knife and, in a circular motion, work out the dirt or scruff that may be imbedded in the skin.

One alternative to this process is to skin the carcass first and then dip it into hot water after the rest of the butchering process is finished.

This will allow you to go directly to dressing the carcass and leave this less-valuable portion for later. The meat is far more valuable than the skin.

THE HUMANE KILL

Now that you have a clean place to work, sturdy tables on which to work, your knives are sharp and your equipment is clean and set out ready to use, you have enough people to assist you and they have been briefed on their tasks, and all the catch tubs are assembled, you are now ready to kill your pig. It is best to read through all the steps needed to process your pig before you begin rather than using this as a read-as-you-go text.

You can obtain a humane kill in three ways: stunning, shooting, and sticking. The first two are the easiest and offer the least safety concerns while the latter method is free of firearms or stunning equipment but also has the most potential for problems.

Stunning involves using a compression gun, which is a handheld device that can have either a long or short handle and can be a penetrating or nonpenetrating type. When a special-purpose blank rifle cartridge is fired inside the handheld stun gun, it activates a solid metal bolt that slams into the brain of the pig, knocking it unconscious so that it feels no further pain but allows for a complete bleed because the heart is still pumping. The stun gun has the advantage of being portable and easy to handle to administer the stunning. Restraint of the pig is essential so that it remains motionless just prior to firing the gun that is positioned on its forehead. To work correctly, the gun must touch the skull at the time it is fired.

Shooting involves using a rifle or small firearm to impel a bullet into the brain, also rendering the pig unconscious. If you use a rifle or small firearm, be sure all safety procedures are followed and that no one is near the animal except yourself. The rifle or small firearm *should not* be touching the skull when discharged because being too close to the hard skull may cause it to backfire and result in injury to you. One disadvantage with shooting the pig is that once it is dead the heart stops and the bleed may not be as complete. You will rely more on gravity to drain most of the blood from the carcass. However, it is a swift kill if done correctly.

Sticking is pushing the point of a knife into the throat to slice the jugular vein to begin the bleeding process. In this case the pig remains alive until enough blood has drained out of its body to stop the heart from beating. This method typically produces the best bleed but has some safety concerns.

In all three methods you will have to lift the pig and suspend it by its hind legs to let gravity help with the bleed. Sticking a pig while it is still standing on all four legs is a difficult maneuver, but not impossible. However, if not done accurately and swiftly, you may only slice its jowl and throat without hitting the jugular vein. This will undoubtedly agitate the pig greatly. And even if you do slice the jugular, in this position you will likely not be able to capture any of the escaping blood for later use.

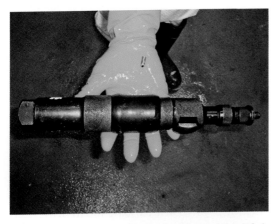

A cartridge discharge stun gun will render the pig unconscious so it feels no pain while the initial cuts are made and the bleeding is done.

Regardless of the method used, you will need sturdy equipment to suspend the pig once it has been killed. A chain or straps can be looped and tightened between the hock and the hoof on the lower part of its two rear legs to hoist it into the air. In this position, the chains or straps will not injure or bruise the hams.

Let's assume that you have shot or stunned the pig and have raised it into the air with chains, straps, or gambrel hooks. You are now ready to slice open the jugular to capture the blood. This may take several minutes and will slowly come to a stop, at which point you can proceed to the next step of opening the belly.

If the pig is suspended while still alive, and this will likely be the method used if sticking the pig to kill it, there are things to be aware of. In this position, the pig has less ability to free itself while hanging upside down than if it is rolled on its back or side and held by your helpers before sticking to kill it. The upside-down position helps immobilize a live pig and will make it easier to complete an effective jugular severance. The most effective bleed occurs when its head hangs downward rather than its whole body lying flat on the floor. However, be aware that a live pig will not find this a comfortable position to be in and will typically flail its front feet. These must be immobilized by firmly holding them on either side or by tying them to a post so they can't be used as weapons by the pig to defend itself.

After safely and sufficiently immobilizing your pig, you can cut the jugular vein. Begin by pressing the sharp blade point against the skin just in front of the breastbone and quickly sliding it into its neck. Then make a short vertical incision about 4 inches long in the center of the neck, followed by a horizontal slice across the inside of its throat to slice the vein. This should sever both veins that run along the esophagus and release large quantities of blood.

Lift the pig's carcass by its hind legs and suspend it for bleeding. After severing the jugular, collect the blood for later use. It must be cooled immediately with salt added to prevent clotting and bacterial growth.

Your tubs should have been placed below the pig's head to catch the escaping blood. Even if you have no plans for the blood later, using tubs will make the area easier to clean up. Remember that a pig's total weight is about 7 percent blood. The example we used earlier of a 240-pound pig will yield about 17 pounds of blood. Not all the blood will drain completely from its body. About 60 percent will be recovered, and between 20 to 25 percent may still be retained in the heart and internal organs. Up to as much as 10 percent of the blood volume can be retained in the muscle tissue throughout its body.

Do not insert the knife point too far into the neck when you make your first incision. You do not want it to pass into the chest cavity because this will cause blood to seep into it. Also, do not stick the pig in its heart to kill it. You want the heart to continue pumping as long as possible, and it will do so for a time after the pig is unconscious.

The key to this phase is to get a good bleed as quickly as possible. When the blood flow has stopped or slowed to a drip, your pig can be moved to a table where it can be skinned, which, as mentioned, requires less time and effort to remove than scalding it.

The main problem associated with collecting blood is to prevent the contamination by bacteria from the skin. Coagulation can be prevented by the addition of cold water and anticoagulants, such as citric acid, sodium citrate, or salt. Also, the fibrin that binds blood clots together can be removed by vigorous stirring with a large spoon.

REMOVE FEET FIRST

You can remove the four feet before lifting the carcass. To remove the front feet, begin by making a circular cut at a point just below the back side of the knee joint. Cut all the way through the remaining skin until you reach bone. Severing these tendons will allow you to break the knee joint forward, snapping it. Then cut completely through the exposed joint to sever the foot. Do the same with the other front foot and place them in a tub for later work.

For the rear legs, you do not want to cut through those tendons because you want them intact to lift the carcass. However, you can make circular cuts around the bottom of the hock joint until you reach bone. Snap the leg bone back against its normal position and it will crack open slightly. Then cut through the joint to remove the bottom part of the leg. Then do the same for the other rear leg and you should have two exposed rear leg joints with intact tendons.

There is a slight indentation between the tendons and the bone on each rear leg. This is located just above the joint you cut off. Using your knife, carefully make a 3-inch-long slit, keeping your blade tipped toward the bone so as not to cut the tendon. Then slip the gambrel ends through each slit and you are ready to lift the carcass.

A gambrel is often used to suspend a carcass. This is a long metal rod that is slipped between the tendon and the rear leg bone of each hind leg. These tendons are strong enough to hold the heavy carcass if they haven't been cut.

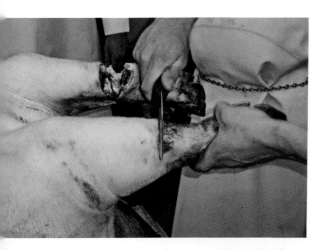

Begin the carcass deconstruction by removing the front and rear feet. Make a deep cut down to the bone on the backside of the knee joint.

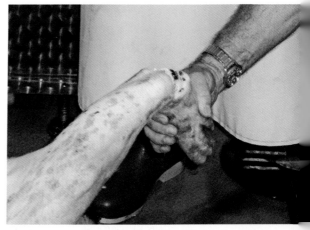

After making the cut, push down on the feet and crack the joint open. Then sever the skin with your knife to remove the feet.

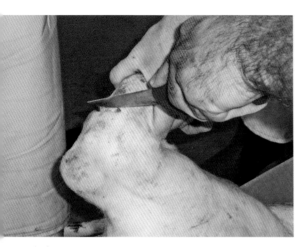

Make a deep cut on the hind leg joint just below the hock. Cutting at this spot will allow you to snap it open to separate the joint and then to sever the skin while keeping the tendon intact for lifting the carcass.

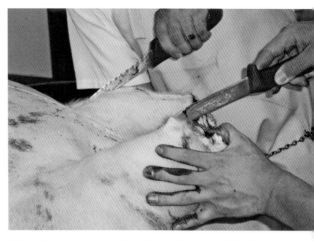

To begin skinning the carcass, lift the skin and slice down each front leg to the chest.

SKINNING

Removing the hide by skinning it takes off the outer layer without the need to use hot, boiling water for scalding or the extra effort of scraping off the hair.

Most people who home butcher have little need for the skin, which is often discarded. In the past, the skin was left on the hams as they were processed and cured, but with modern refrigeration this is not necessary. It will not add flavor, but it will protect the hams and bacon from drying out too quickly.

The easiest way to skin a pig is to lay the carcass on a table or V-shaped trolley or suspend it

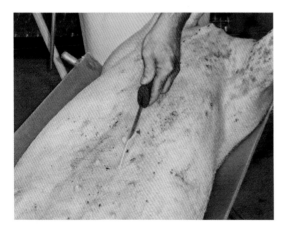

Then score a line down the center, from the chest to the pelvis, but don't cut into the abdomen. This will allow you to peel away the skin while keeping the internal organs intact.

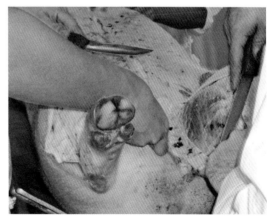

Make a slice on the inside of each rear leg to the center line cut of the belly. Begin to slice the skin as if you were peeling an orange.

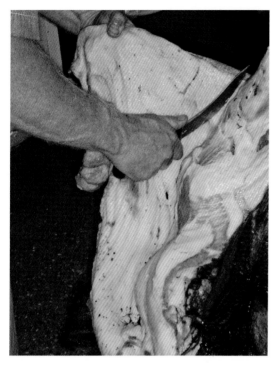

Continue skinning the sides by making slow, sweeping cuts, pulling the skin away as you slice. Avoid cutting into the muscles as it is better to leave a little more fat on the carcass than to slice into it.

vertically at an appropriate work height. Skinning the carcass is like peeling an orange. You want to remove the outside without injuring the inside. As you begin to remove the skin, do not open up or cut into the abdomen, or cut into the muscles.

Begin your first cuts at the rear ankles with a short skinning knife. Slice completely around them, but avoid cutting the tendons above the hocks. These tendons will be used shortly for helping to suspend the carcass. If they are cut through, you will need to find another means to hold the carcass in the air.

After your circling slices are done, make cuts down the inside center of each rear leg to a point below the pelvis, all the while avoiding cutting into the muscles. Do the same for the front legs and cut to a center point at the base of the chest. Score a line down the center of the belly with your knife, from the anus to the base of the chest, but *do not* cut through the abdominal wall.

Start the skinning at the chest and pull the skin away from the body with one hand while you slice the connection tissue with your other hand.

The skin can be removed from the head if it hasn't already been cut off. Trim off any meat that may be attached and set it aside for sausage making.

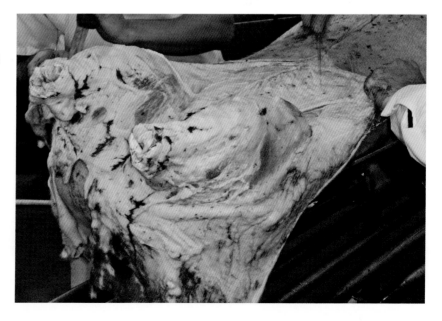

You can remove the skin entirely while it is on the table or raise the carcass and finish the skin removal while hanging.

The tension of pulling will help separate the skin from the body.

Complete the skinning of the front and rear legs and then start on the belly. Turn the knife blade out, away from the abdomen, and lift the skin as you slice down the center line from one end to the other. Then make slow, sweeping motions between the skin and body to separate them. Do one side first and then the other. Continue until the entire skin is completely removed. It can then be set aside.

HANGING THE CARCASS

At this point, you will need to suspend the carcass vertically for several practical reasons:

- It will be easier to open the abdomen and eviscerate the carcass.

- It will allow residual blood to drain out.

- It will allow easier splitting of the carcass.

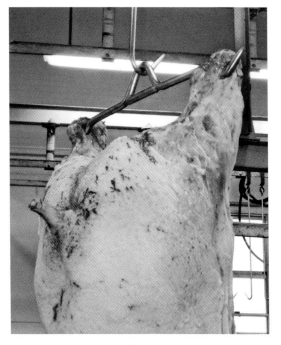

Lift the carcass by using a gambrel. Make cuts between the rear leg tendons and the bone and then slip the gambrel tips through each rear leg to lift it.

With the skin now removed, you can make a slit through the tissue surrounding the tendon and leg and push the gambrel end through it. After you do the same with the other leg, you are ready to lift the carcass. Be sure the legs are secure and can't slip off the gambrel, causing the carcass to fall to the floor. Once the carcass is fully suspended, you are now ready to open up the body cavity.

Removing the internal organs is easier if the pig is suspended. You can use gravity to assist you in ways you can't if it is lying flat on a table. Plus, it will help drain residual blood that did not initially escape from the sticking. Any residual blood will pool in the tissues if it remains flat on a table before cooling.

HEAD FIRST

You need to remove the head first. This accomplishes two things: It gets it out of the way for working with the rest of the evisceration, and it aids in cooling down the carcass because heat will escape once it's removed. And it will help with draining any residual blood pooling in the neck.

Begin removing the head by making a cut above the ears at the first joint of the backbone, and then across the back of the neck. As you cut

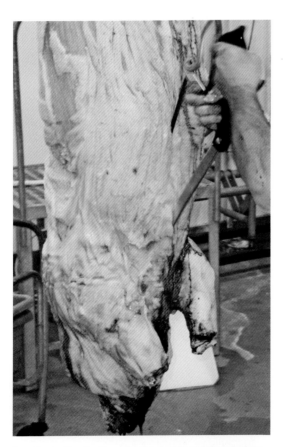

Open the chest by using the meat saw and cut through the breastbone but not into the abdominal cavity. This cut will allow blood to drain out that has been pooling while lying on the table.

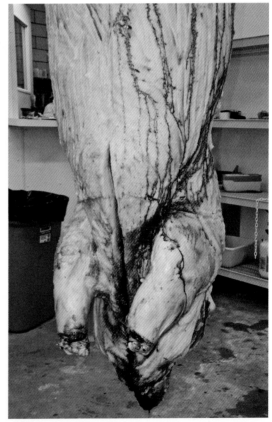

Your chest cut should look something like this after using the meat saw or a sturdy knife.

through the windpipe and throat, the head will drop down, but don't slice the head completely off just yet.

Pull down on the ears and continue your cut around the ears to the eyes and then toward the point of the jawbone, unless you want the head for roasting or headcheese. Then do not make this last cut.

The head will come free when you slice through the last part of the skin at the end of the jaw, although the skin of the jowls will still hold it. Slice through this skin and the head will be severed.

You should have a clean tarp or plastic covering on the floor even if it gets blood dripped on it. The head will be heavy and in an awkward position for you to catch after the skin is sliced through and no longer holding it. The head can weigh up to 20 pounds. Be careful of grabbing the head by its jaw as the teeth can be sharp. Once the head is completely loose, you can rinse it off and work with it later. Place it in an ice-filled tub if you have it available, and this will help cool it down.

CARCASS SPLITTING

The process of splitting the carcass in half begins by scoring a line down the center of the belly with your knife, but don't cut into the belly wall. Start your line at a point between the hams and run the line down to the base of the chest.

You will want to split open the breastbone first. Do this by inserting the heel of your knife against the bone and cutting outward. You may have to work or wiggle the blade as you apply outward pressure, being careful not to let your blade slip. If your knife will not cut through the breastbone, you can use your meat saw.

Whether using a knife or saw, be careful not to cut past the upper portion of the breastbone and into the stomach, which, because the carcass is hanging, will have settled closer to it on the inside. Gravity will be pulling all of the internal organs

toward the breastbone and first rib, and you do not want to cut the stomach open because this will release its gastric contents inside the body cavity. Opening the breastbone will allow pooled blood that has accumulated to drain out.

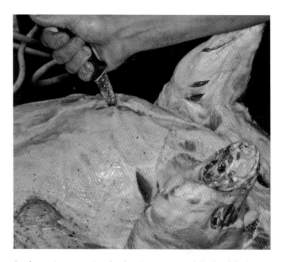

An alternative to opening the chest is to use a sturdy knife while the carcass is still on the table. Insert it just behind the breastbone and pull toward the neck to crack open the cavity. This will also allow the blood to drain after the carcass has been lifted.

To open the abdomen, make a small cut in the soft cavity between the rear legs to gain access with your hand to the small intestine connecting to the anus.

Use heavy string to tie off the small intestine tightly so that it will not slip off after the intestines are removed from the interior cavity.

You can now make an incision in the abdominal wall, near the top of the rear part of the carcass to begin the evisceration. Pull the skin outward with your fingers and make a 4-inch-long slit into the body wall. This will allow you access to the inside of the belly without cutting into the intestines. The intestines do not adhere to the abdomen, so they will not be near this cut. Since all the internal organs will be pulled downward, this cut will allow you to slide your hand into the abdomen along with your knife to cut all the way down without injuring the internal organs. But before doing this, make sure your hands, arms, and knife have been cleaned with soap and water.

There is a simple trick to enter the abdomen with your hand and knife. Pull the slit outward with your free hand. Grip the handle of the knife with the blade turned toward you and away from the internal organs. Basically you will be holding the knife backwards. The reason for this will become quickly apparent.

As you slowly slice downward, the heel of your knife blade should be right against the inside of the body and your pointed blade completely sticking outward toward you. Be careful that you have good footing and don't slip while in this position. Holding the knife in this position will allow you to cut down the belly and away from the internal organs without nicking or puncturing them. As you slice down the belly, use the backside of your wrist and forearm, holding the knife, to push the internal organs back into the cavity to keep them away from the blade. It may feel awkward at first, but it will prove useful. You will experience more pressure against your knife hand the closer you get to the bottom because of the accumulation of all the internal parts at the bottom of the cavity.

As you slice down the belly and reach the split breastbone, the intestines will fall forward and downward. However, they will still be attached by muscle fiber and will not fall completely out. This evisceration method is easier and poses less risk to accidentally cutting into the stomach, organs, or intestines than drawing the knife upward to slice the belly open.

A clean tub should be placed under the carcass to catch the viscera as you pull the kidneys, heart, liver, and stomach toward the opening. At this point, the intestines are still suspended by the gut leading to the anus.

SPLIT THE AITCHBONE

You will want to split the aitchbone, or pelvic bone next, but before you do, take some heavy cotton cord or string and firmly tie shut the

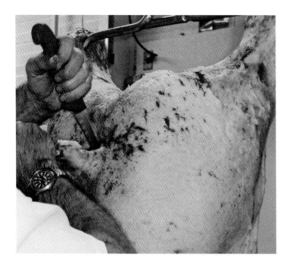

After tying off the intestine, make a circular cut around the anus muscle below the tail until it slips free of the pelvis.

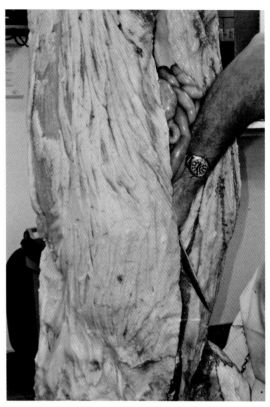

Turn the knife blade toward you and place the heel against the skin of the belly. Then slowly slice downward and push the intestine and internal organs back with your hand and forearm.

As you slice downward, the internal organs will spill outward but not completely as they will be held by the internal connective tissues.

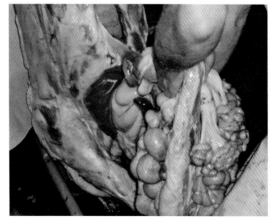

Once the kidneys and connective tissues are cut, the internal mass will then fall out. Hold firmly as you pull it into the tub below and cut the esophagus to fully remove it from the carcass.

intestine end nearest the anus. This will keep any fecal material from falling out once you excise the anal muscle.

You will need to split the aitchbone in half to separate the hips and make the cut down the spine easier to split the carcass.

Use your knife to cut through the skin and small muscles between the hams until you reach the aitchbone. You may be able to use the heel of a heavy knife to cut through or you may need to use a meat saw. If you use a knife, you may need to wiggle the blade to pass it through the joint, but be careful not to cut so far through the bone that it slips and slices into the anus.

Once the bone is split, use your knife and make a circular cut around the anus muscle until it is

Use a heavy mesh butcher's glove on your free hand to prevent accidental cuts. Always wash and disinfect the glove before and after use. They are reversible and can be used on either hand.

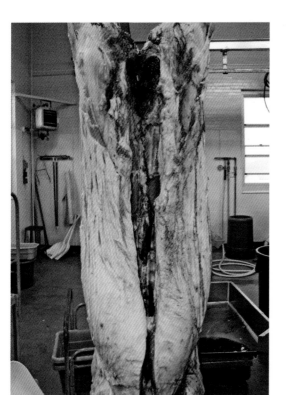

The carcass will be an empty cavity after all the internal organs and intestines are removed. It is now ready to be split in half.

free from the bone. Once it is loose from the pelvis, it will be the last restraining hold on the internal organs, which will then collapse down toward your tub. This will happen very quickly once that last cut is made. The entire intestinal mass will slip out of the body cavity, and this is the reason it is so important to securely tie off the anal opening before cutting it loose.

After the viscera drops, the diaphragm will now be exposed, and you will see the gullet that leads to the stomach. Tie it off with a heavy cotton cord or string, like you did the anus, and then sever it. The entire mass of viscera now should be free to drop into the tub.

Sharing the butchering tasks will make the work easier and more efficient. Once the viscera is removed, the person designated to work with it should place it all on a clean table to cut out the liver and wash it with clean, cold water. Trim out the gall bladder and remove the spleen. The stomach should be tied off at both ends and cut free. The intestines should be placed in a separate tub as they will need to be washed of all fecal matter and placed in a salt brine for use with sausage making.

At this point, the heart and lungs will still be inside the carcass cavity and lying in front of the diaphragm. Make an incision where the red muscle joins the connective tissue to expose the heart and lungs. These should be pulled downward and cut free from the backbone. Trim any fat off the heart and lungs and wash them with cold water.

Healthy internal organs will have bright colors and a firm texture. Examine all the organs for any abnormalities or lesions before using them. Place them all in clean ice water until you are ready to work with them. Slicing open these organs, except the intestines, will help remove heat and blood.

SPLIT THE BACKBONE

You are now ready to make the final split of the full carcass. Wash down the inside of the carcass cavity with clean, cold water before making any further cuts. This will rinse out any foreign matter and keep it from contaminating the meat once cut.

You can use a heavy blade or a hand or electric meat saw to divide the carcass into two pieces. Start at the top where you split open the aitchbone and slice down the center of the spine. Be sure to make a straight cut so you don't damage the loins. Continue until you reach the bottom and separate the carcass into two halves. It is now ready for cooling or processing.

COOLING THE CARCASS

It is easier to trim and cut up a chilled carcass than a warm one. Cooling it quickly also minimizes bacterial growth and souring of the meat.

You will need a separate vat or tub large enough to submerge the two halves of the carcass completely, or two tubs and put one half in each. Since you have not cut into any muscle yet, the contamination risk is low. You are cooling the muscles down and need ice to do this or have access to a large refrigerated unit. You can use a freezer, but freezing the meat is different from

chilling it. Unless you can change the settings to between 34º to 38ºF, this is not recommended. If, however, you can set the temperature between them, then you can use it as a refrigeration unit, if the carcass will fit completely inside it to close the lid. Or, if only one half will fit, the other can be placed in an ice bath. If ice is used, submerge the carcass for a minimum of twenty-four hours to ensure thorough chilling. You should monitor the bath and replenish the ice as it melts. It will draw out the heat from the muscles.

You should not cut up the carcass until all the tissue heat is gone. When it is thoroughly chilled, you are ready to deconstruct the carcass.

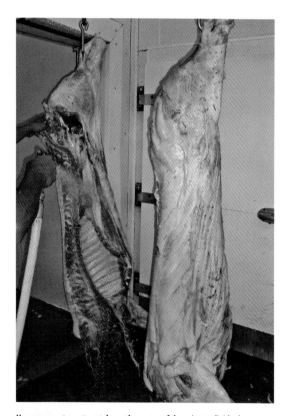

Use your meat saw to cut down the center of the spine to divide the carcass. Make a straight cut so that you don't cut into the loin areas. After splitting it, rinse the carcass with clean water, inside and outside, to remove residual blood, bone dust, and any foreign matter. It is now ready to be cooled.

Chapter 3

WHERE PORK MEAT COMES FROM

In simple terms, the muscles of the animal are the meat. The muscles are the numerous bundles of cells and fibers that can be contracted and expanded to produce the body's movements. The three major types of muscles are the skeletal, cardiac, and smooth.

Skeletal muscles are linked to bone by bundles of collagen fibers known as tendons. The skeletal muscles are made up of several components referred to as muscle fibers. These fibers bundle together in various configurations that give them a striated appearance, such as grooves or parallel lines that may overlap in different directions. These fibers form the basic mechanism that controls muscle contraction.

Muscles contract; they never push because the fibers are too soft to propel bone forward. The animal's body is constructed in such a way that when one muscle contracts an opposing muscle will relax, allowing movement. When both muscles relax at the same time, no movement occurs. And the location of these muscles will largely determine the amount of use they get.

While the skeletal muscles support the body structure and initiate movement, smooth muscles are found in the organs or the tubular system, such as the digestive tract, reproductive organs, circulatory system, and urinary tract. Lastly, the cardiac muscle is found in the heart.

From a carcass value perspective, skeletal muscles are the most important of the three types because of their quantity and desirability for human consumption.

This chapter will examine the major muscles found in a pig, how to identify them when you cut up a carcass, how to cut them into the most useable portions, and what to do with some of the less edible parts. Understanding the muscle terrain of your pig carcass will help you when cutting it up and dividing it into portions.

PIG MUSCLES AND BONES

More than 100 different muscles are found in a pig's body. For general use, however, they are usually grouped into five major areas and then further broken down into specialty cuts, often depending on their marketing characteristics or potential.

This is what you will encounter when you begin deconstructing the carcass, also referred to as the fabrication process. This process will break down large portions of one area into smaller, more manageable pieces or cuts.

The five major areas include the shoulder (picnic and Boston butt), loin, hams, and belly or sides. The minor areas include the head, cheek and jowl, and the feet and hocks.

The five major divisions of a carcass can be further broken down into eleven sections, which will help identify the muscles and bones in that portion and allow us to discuss them in detail. While this only describes one-half of the carcass, you will remember that there will be an identical section on the other half; the two halves are mirror images of each other. We'll start with the bones as they can be trimmed and used for soup stock or, in some cases, pickled.

- **Tarsal bone**—from the rear hock down to the toes. Each rear leg has seven bones. They are short, cubical bones of various sizes. It is sometimes called the hock joint. Two dewclaws suspend from the metatarsal bones in each rear foot.

- **Tibia**—are located just above the rear hock and below the femur, or the stifle. Pigs have two tibia bones, one located in each hind leg. It has a distinctive curve in the bone shaft. This is commonly referred to as the rear leg bone, hind shank, or hock bone.

- **Femur**—lies anterior (in front of) the tibia and below the hind leg, and it is often called the round bone or leg bone. There is only one in each hind leg. It is the largest and most massive of the long bones and has a larger shape at the top and bottom than of the cylindrical shaft. It also has a flat shape on the posterior (behind) side.

- **Pelvis**—made up of four different bone structures: the ischium, or aitchbone; the pubis; the coccygeal; and sacral vertebrae (often melded together in any reference as the tail).

  - The *ischium* or *aitchbone* consists of one pair. This means they are fused together with tendons and tissue and are mirror images of each other—one found on each side of an imaginary center line. Although they slope slightly downward and inward, they are almost horizontal when viewed from the side.

  - The *pelvic girdle* consists of three parts and the pubis is the smallest. It forms the forward part of the pelvic floor and, like the ischium, consists of one pair of bones.

- The *tailbone* consists of the twenty coccygeal vertebrae. These lie from the very tip of the tail to the sacral vertebrae nearest the pelvis.

- The *sacral vertebrae* consists of five fused vertebrae that are irregularly shaped. Because they are fused, they are often described as one bone—the sacrum. They attach to the lumbar vertebrae rather than the pubis bone.

- **Lumbar vertebrae**—often called the loin or lower back. The lower back position refers to the direction from the nose horizontally and not vertically. Pigs have six irregularly shaped bones in number, and they attach to the thoracic vertebrae in front and the sacral vertebrae in back.

- **Thoracic vertebrae**—form the part in front of the loin or lower back and up to the neck. This includes the shoulder area as they are referred to as the *chine* or *featherbone*, or *rib vertebrae*. The rib bones attach the thoracic vertebrae as they suspend downward.

- **Ribs**—consist of thirteen elongated and curved bones. They are arranged in pairs with one pair of the ribs (whole carcass) for each thoracic vertebrae. The first eight pairs fuse to the sternum and the other five attach to the thoracic vertebrae.

- **Scapula**—consists of one pair. It is referred to as the *shoulder blade*, *blade bone*, or the *paddle bone* because of its shape. It is a flat, smooth bone that attaches to the humerus only on the forward end. The rear part is not attached to any bone but is tied to muscles and tendons, which help facilitate a forward and backward front leg movement.

- **Cervical vertebrae**—also called the neck bones. Pigs have seven irregularly shaped bones of varying sizes. They attach at the skull at the front end and the thoracic vertebrae at the rear end.

- **Humerus**—or *arm bone*, is a single pair—one on each front leg—that extends from the shoulder down to the foreshank. It is a curved bone or shape, being larger at the top near the scapula and smaller near the foreshank. It looks like a backward *S* shape.

- **Radius,** or **foreshank bone**—the largest of the two forearm bones. It is gently curved and extends from the humerus to the metacarpal bones and is tied to the ulna, which lies right below it (behind it if viewed vertically).

- **Ulna**—also referred to as the foreshank bone and consists of one in each front leg. Like the radius, it is a long bone that extends from the humerus to the metacarpal bones of the lower leg. It lies behind or posterior to the radius and has a three-sided shaft.

- **Metacarpal bones** or **cannon bones**—lie below the knee to the front feet. Pigs have five bones in this point, but they are referred to as *long bones*. Two dewclaws descend from the metacarpal bones in each front foot.

- **Carpal bones**—found in the front legs and consist of six bones, which are arranged in two rows closest to the attachment point, consisting of four bones. In the farthest row, the second and third bones are fused and the fourth is separate.

- **Skull**—the head and consists of the cranium, which houses the brains; the mandible, or lower jaw, which works by muscle action for eating; and the sinuses, through which air flows to the lungs.

- **Phalanges**—the front and rear feet. They consist of three separate, relatively long and narrow bones.

- **Hoof**—not a bone but a covering that forms a protection over the lowest leg bones. The hooves act as shock absorbers to reduce the impact of the foot against any surface. They are made mostly of keratin and modified epidermal cells. The **dewclaws** do not have any practical purpose but can be skinned and boiled with bones for soup stock.

MUSCLES ARE MEAT

The skeleton supports the muscles, which are attached to the various bones by tendons and connective tissue. As long as the bone doesn't break or the muscles don't tear because of injury, the normal functions of the pig's metabolic system will allow the muscles to expand and develop volume as the pig gets older.

These bones support movement, and although there are many divisions of the bones, there are also many divisions of the muscles to make that movement happen. Some muscles will get more use because of the bone they are attached to. For example, leg bones move more than the back bones so the shoulder muscles are more active than the loin muscles.

We can use the muscle divisions and divide the cuts into sections and identify their composition and how they can best be used. These can be classified generally as thoracic muscles, abdominal muscles, thigh muscles, and shoulder and neck muscles.

- **Thoracic muscles** are dominated by the pectoral muscles, both front and rear of the foreleg. These provide forward and backward movement. There is a broad muscle just behind the front legs that, even though it's smaller, gives the foreleg great power for movement because of its length.

- **Abdominal muscles** help compress the abdominal wall and protect the internal organs from injury. Unlike the chest and lungs, the abdomen is not protected by skeletal bones. The internal organs are held in place by the pressure of the long abdominal muscles, which also help flex the trunk for turning. Pigs have three abdominal layers: the external and internal oblique, and the transverse muscle.

  - The *external oblique* is a thin broad sheet of muscle covering the lower length of the abdomen.

  - The *internal oblique* runs in an opposite direction of the upper layer.

  - The *transverse muscle* is the innermost of the abdominal muscle layers.

The arrangement of the three layers gives the abdominal wall its strength. Because these are thin muscle layers and are well interspersed with fat deposits, they are difficult to trim out. Since this is where bacon comes from, they can be cut differently from other more voluminous muscles.

- **Thigh muscles** are large and contain the well-known hams. The femoral artery passes between the layers.

- **Shoulder and neck muscles** are prominent and extend from the back of the neck and jaw, and the back of the head through the shoulder to the humerus bone. The *brachiocephalic muscle* is a single muscle that attaches from the neck to the jaw and helps to raise and lower the mouth while eating.

These major muscle groups will be broken down later into specific muscle cuts, but for now this information will help you identify their general location. Once you begin to fabricate or cut up the carcass and deconstruct it into smaller cuts or pieces, you can keep this overview in mind. While it is not necessary to become an anatomical expert of a pig's muscle structure, it will help you understand what the major areas are composed of.

MOVEMENT MAKES MUSCLE

As with any other animal used for meat, the most tender cuts or muscles are those that don't get the most exercise or movement, such as the loin area, from which pork chops and pork loin are derived. Those muscles that get more use, such as the shoulders and hams, tend to have a higher bone-to-lean meat ratio than other cuts. This doesn't mean they are less tender, although that is often the case with pigs raised on pasture or in open lots because they get more exercise than those raised in confinement systems. It usually means they need to be cooked differently than more tender cuts.

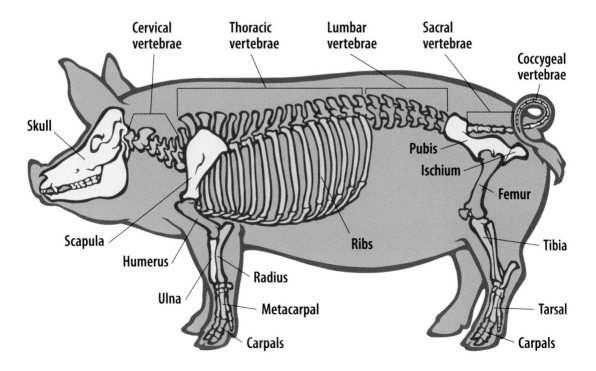

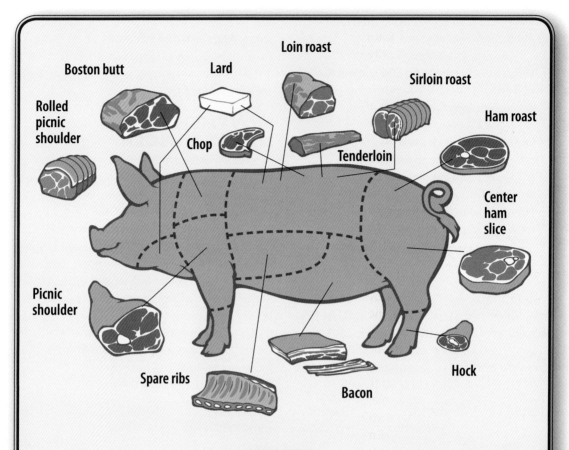

Boston butt

Rolled picnic shoulder

Lard

Loin roast

Sirloin roast

Ham roast

Chop

Tenderloin

Center ham slice

Picnic shoulder

Spare ribs

Bacon

Hock

PORK CHART

Roast
Sirloin roast
Tenderloin
Canadian-style bacon
Loin roast, ham end
Loin roast, center cut
Loin roast, shoulder end
Boston butt
Half ham, butt end
Half ham, shank end
Fresh ham roast
Spare ribs
Fresh picnic shoulder
Smoked picnic shoulder
Rolled picnic shoulder

Pan-Broil
Ham
Loin
Spare ribs
Jowl
Bacon
Center ham slice
Bacon

Fry
Tenderloin
Canadian-style bacon
Chops
Rib pork chop
Frenched chop
Butterfly chop
Center ham slice

Braise
Tenderloin
Chops
Rib pork chop
Frenched chop
Butterfly chop
Spare ribs

Broil
Canadian-style bacon
Bacon

Stew
Half ham, shank end
Smoked picnic shoulder
Fresh shoulder hock

Pork cuts can be deboned or the bone left on when making cuts. This will be a personal preference. Although the majority of cuts found in the retail meat counters today are boneless, you will likely find that it is easier and quicker to deconstruct a carcass and get it into the freezer if each piece is not deboned. But if you have the help, time, talent, and dexterity, you may want to debone every cut. Bones can add flavor to the cut, especially in stews or moist cooking.

The two charts will tell you where the muscle is located and the bones involved. Knowing these names and locations will help you do a better job of carving up the carcass. There is no right or wrong way to cut up a carcass with home butchering since it will be for your family's use and not for sale. The following methods described are only one option, and you can use it as a guide or create your own.

FOOD SAFETY

Before you dive into cutting up the carcass, you need to be aware of one principle that applies to all meat processing: the more you break down a carcass into smaller units, the more risk there is for bacterial exposure and contamination. As more muscle tissue becomes exposed to the environment around it, the risk and opportunity for bacteria to attach and grow increases.

A whole carcass has the minimum amount of exposed surface area. As large cuts are made, more area is exposed. When it is cut into smaller pieces, still more area is exposed. Simply put, the more meat is processed, the more it may be exposed to microorganisms. Using clean, sanitary equipment; clean table surfaces; and keeping work area temperatures low while working as quickly as possible will help reduce microbial activity.

This is the primary reason you need to keep in mind the three Cs. You need to keep it Cold, Clean, and Covered. There's one additional C I

like to include as well: keeping meat separate to prevent Cross-contamination.

KEEP IT CLEAN

Let's start with keeping things clean. Strict sanitation is required before and after cutting any meat and processing it to prevent bacterial contamination and food-borne illnesses. It is especially important to handle raw meat in a sanitary environment to reduce the risk of bacterial growth while it is at room temperature. No meat is completely sterile, but using proper procedures will minimize your risks.

Once everything is ready, it's a good idea to thoroughly wash your hands with soap and water before touching any meat or clean work surfaces. Remove any rings, jewelry, or other metal objects from your hands, ears, or other exposed body parts before cutting meat. Always rewash your hands between tasks, as well as if you come into contact with anything unsanitary: if you sneeze, use the bathroom, or handle materials not part of meat processing, you should rewash your hands.

KEEP IT COLD

Mismanagement of temperature is one of the most common reasons for outbreaks of food-borne diseases. Bacteria grow best at temperatures between 40° and 140°F, so it is important that your fresh pork passes through this range quickly. Meat can be kept safe when it is hot or when it is cold, but not in between. It is best if the meat passes through this temperature range, whether being cooked or cooled, within four hours, but preferably less.

Store your raw meat in a refrigerator until you begin processing it. During the processing of most meat products, it will be essential to reach an internal temperature of 160°F, as this effectively kills pathogenic bacteria. (Most, but not all, microorganisms are killed at 140°F.) The less time you subject the meat to room or ambient temperatures the less risk there will be in it harboring harmful microorganisms that cause spoilage.

If meat is stored below 40°F, most of it can be kept safe from harmful bacteria for a short time. When frozen, most microorganisms that are present are merely dormant and can revive when thawed. If you have frozen the meat, it all should be processed as soon as possible and not refrozen to use later.

KEEP IT COVERED

One simple rule to acknowledge is that all foods have a diminishing shelf life after being opened or made, even if properly stored. However, you can lessen the effects on stored foods created by temperature, the type of wrapping used, and proper storage. The manner in which you cover, contain, or wrap foods prior to use and for storing will help determine how well they keep in a refrigerator, cupboard, or freezer.

Temperature will have the greatest effect on meat, especially as it increases. As previously mentioned, raw or cooked meat should be kept chilled until used. Even your refrigerator will not have consistent temperatures throughout. Interior drawers tend to have slightly higher temperatures than shelves. The door shelves are also generally warmer because of their exposure to room temperatures once they are opened. It is better not to store highly perishable foods such as meat in the drawers or doors of your refrigerator.

PREVENTING CROSS-CONTAMINATION

Cross-contamination occurs when one food comes in contact with another and has the potential of spreading bacteria from one source to another. This can take the form of several variations: both can be raw or one can be raw and one cooked. Cross-contamination could be between meats, vegetables, seafood,

Avoiding Cross-Contamination

- Always wash your hands thoroughly with warm, soapy water prior to, during, and after handling raw pork and other foods. Make sure all counters, cutting boards, plates, knives, and other utensils are thoroughly washed and dried with clean towels.

- Separate different foods into different dishes, plates, or bowls prior to use.

- Keep raw pork, poultry, seafood, or eggs on the bottom shelf of your refrigerator and in sealed containers or bags so they cannot leak or drip onto another food.

- Use a clean cutting board for each of the different foods you are working with. Use a separate board for raw pork, vegetables, and other foods. If you are using the same knives or equipment for all your cutting and processing, make certain to wash them thoroughly each time you move from one food to another or from one cutting surface to another. Replace any cutting boards that have cracks, holes, or grooves as these are good places for bacteria to hide and grow.

- Clean your refrigerator shelves on a regular basis, and particularly if juices from raw pork, vegetables, or seafood have leaked, dripped, or spilled.

- Try to avoid mixing raw meat, vegetables, seafood, and eggs in the same bags when you check out at the grocery store. Try to separate frozen and fresh food into separate bags.

- Never place cooked food on a plate that was used for raw pork, poultry, seafood, or eggs.

eggs, or poultry, or it can occur when surfaces have had mutual contact, such as placing one food on a plate, counter, or cutting board, removing it, and then placing another food on the same surface without washing the surface in between. It can also occur between knives that have not been cleaned between uses and even in your grocery cart if juices happen to leak from one package to another. You can take several steps to avoid cross-contamination of pork or any other foods.

PREVENTING AND RETARDING BACTERIAL GROWTH

Although sanitation and the three (or four) Cs dynamics are routine components of pork processing, misuse or incomplete application of any one of them can be detrimental. Preventing and retarding the development of harmful organisms should be your primary objective while handling raw pork. Consuming microorganisms that have grown and propagated in meat can cause serious illness or even death. This concern should not be taken lightly. When health problems surface relating to eating meat products, it is generally a result of intoxication or infection.

Intoxication occurs when the heating or processing fails to kill the microbes in question. Those that are able to survive can produce a toxin that, when eaten by humans, can produce illness. One example is undercooked meat. Infection occurs when an organism such as salmonella or listeria is consumed due to contamination.

Several types of toxins exist, including exotoxins and endotoxins. Exotoxins are located outside of the bacterial cell and are composed of proteins that can be destroyed by heat through cooking. Exotoxins are among the most poisonous substances known to humans. These include *Clostridium botulinum*, which causes tetanus and botulism poisoning.

Endotoxins attach to the outer membranes of cells but are not released unless the cell is disrupted. These are complex fat and carbohydrate molecules, such as *Staphylococcus aureus*, that are not destroyed by heat.

Bacteria are the most common and important organisms that can grow on meat. Not all bacteria are bad, however, as according to a 2007 New York University study, the human body may carry as many as 180 different kinds of bacteria on its surface. Although molds and yeasts can affect meat quality and cause spoilage, their effect is far less significant or life threatening than toxins or bacteria. Molds typically cause spoilage in grains, cereals, flour, and nuts that have low moisture content or in fruits that have a low pH. Yeasts will not have a significant effect on meat because of the low sugar or carbohydrate content of muscle. They need high sugar and carbohydrate levels to affect a change.

Several parasites may cause a problem if the pork is undercooked or improperly processed. A parasite infection will occur in the live animal before it occurs in a human. There is one swine-related parasite that you should be aware of. This includes *Trichinella spiralis*. Trichinosis is a parasite that can live in swine muscle and may be transferred to humans through raw or undercooked pork. Using and maintaining recommended cooking temperatures and times will destroy these parasites.

MOISTURE AND OXYGEN

Moisture in meat is essential for palatability, but it is also a medium for microbial growth. The level of moisture in fresh pork is high enough to provide spoilage organisms with an ideal environment for growth. Researchers have found that moisture levels of at least 18 percent will allow molds to grow in meat. Drying meats through a smoking or cooking process will typically eliminate any concerns with moisture.

Oxygen is necessary for animals to survive but is an unwelcome agent when processing pork. Yeasts and molds are aerobic microbes that need oxygen to grow. Anaerobic microbes grow when oxygen is present, and this group can be deadly because it includes clostridium, which produces a toxin, and a group called putrifiers, which degrade proteins and produce foul-smelling gases.

Drying is one procedure to follow when processing pork because it acts as an inhibitor of enzyme action by removing moisture. When moisture is removed, enzymes cannot efficiently contact or react with the meat fibers or particles. Without this interaction, bacteria, fungal spores, or naturally occurring enzymes from the raw meat cannot grow to proportions that can cause severe illness. Minute traces may still be present, but with no growth, they lie dormant. However, lying dormant does not mean they can't resume growth if moisture or temperature conditions are introduced that are favorable to them.

MUSCLES AND MOLECULAR TRANSFORMATION

Muscles are meat, and their texture and the fats found in the bodies of pigs are largely reflective of their diets.

The position of the muscles on the skeleton has a significant impact on the texture of meat. For example, muscles that create movement, such as the front and hindquarters in pigs, receive more exercise than the loin or belly areas. The more exercise or movement a muscle uses, the more blood flow is needed. This, in turn, creates a darker color meat because of the flow of hemoglobin, which delivers oxygen to the muscle. The more hemoglobin (sometimes referred to as myoglobin) a muscle contains, the darker color the muscle will be.

The muscles of a harvested pig go through a molecular transformation once the heart stops. This can influence the muscle texture. With the cessation of blood and oxygen flow, the muscle pH begins to gradually drop. This occurs because the glycogen reserves within the animal's muscles are depleted and then converted to lactic acid. Because oxygen is no longer available to the muscle cells, lactic acid levels rise, the pH begins to drop, and the reserves of creatine phosphates diminish.

Creatine phosphates aid in muscle movement, and when they are no longer available, the muscle filaments can no longer slide over one another and the muscle becomes still and rigid, resulting in a condition known as rigor mortis.

Soon after your pig is harvested, the muscle undergoes a gradual change in pH and will decline from a normal pH of 7.0 to 5.5. This decline results from a loss of glycogen held within the muscle and its conversion to lactic acid. The degree of acidity or alkalinity (pH) will have an effect on the growth of microorganisms. Most of these will thrive at a pH that is nearly neutral (7.0) than at any other level above or below it. Meat pH can range from 4.8 to 6.8, but microorganisms generally grow slower at a pH of 5.0 or below. This acidity level can act as a preservative in some instances and is generally not a concern unless there is a long delay in processing the carcass at room temperatures.

The amount of time it takes a pig's muscles to reach their final pH levels are influenced by several factors. These include the cooling rate of the carcass and the extent of the animal's struggle at the time of death. Cooling affects the time because metabolism is slowed when the carcass is subjected to lower temperatures. Finally, the animal's activity level immediately prior to the killing will affect the pH, with less activity prolonging the period of pH decline.

Understanding these factors affecting meat quality is not intended to discourage you from processing your own meat. Rather, it is meant to increase your awareness to the potential for problems resulting from mishandling or inadequately processing your pig. Humans have been safely butchering and handling the meat for their families for generations because they understood the basic principles to preserve meat properly.

CALM ANIMAL HANDLING

It is important to handle your animal calmly before slaughter. We've already talked about setting up a pen to place your pig in a day or two before the butchering is scheduled. Reducing its physical stress before slaughter also reduces the chance of adrenaline increasing in its system and affecting the meat quality. The reasoning is simple.

Research shows that animals that are stressed immediately before slaughter call upon glycogen in the muscle and liver to meet muscle energy demands. If a pig is excited or stressed just before you kill it and before the muscle glycogen levels return to normal, the excess glycogen is converted to lactic acid and the pH drops faster than normal, resulting in a pale, lean color.

If your pig is under stress for 24 hours or longer before slaughter, it will likely use up all of its muscle glycogen because of prolonged muscle energy demands. This will result in a lower level of glycogen in the muscle when slaughtered and a lower level of lactic acid in the muscle. The pH will then remain high and the meat will be dark-colored, making it less attractive. Calm, safe handling measures are needed to ensure normal muscle energy demands and to avoid abnormal increases and decreases in pH levels.

TO KEEP BONES OR NOT

There are about as many reasons to keep the bones intact in the meat cut as there are to cut them out. The choice will be yours, and there may be some advantages to leaving them in, such as with cooking pork chops.

When deconstructing the carcass, you will be cutting through various bones to create smaller pieces for cooking, packaging, or storing. Prior to packaging, you may keep the bones in or cut them out. The cuts can be frozen, and when thawed for use at a later date, they can be trimmed of the bone. Cutting out the bones will take more work at butchering time.

The main reason for keeping the bone intact with the meat cut is the flavor and texture it can add to dishes. The marrow on the inside of all bones consists of albumen and collagen, along with blood cells. When heated, these substances release gelatin, which creates flavors for soups, stock, and stews. Leaving bones on the meat helps conduct heat to aid in cooking the cut thoroughly. It also helps prevent the meat from drying out. Boneless meat typically cooks faster than meat on the bone because it doesn't need to heat the bone itself. The choice is yours whether to keep the bones intact or to take them out.

Chapter 4

FARM TO TABLE

The process of raising a pig with the ultimate goal of it reaching your kitchen table as a family meal is the full cycle of animal husbandry. It can be no other way if you commit yourself to raising livestock. By fulfilling its intended destiny, your pig can provide many satisfying meals and good nutrition for your family.

Pork is a highly nutritious protein, and a single pig can yield not only meat but skin for cooking, lard for rendering and then to be used in baking, and many other products. We will look more closely at the meat in this chapter rather than subsidiary products that take more specialized equipment to utilize.

You will have read through all the fabrication steps before you begin to think about a date for butchering your pig. You will have thought through all the steps that will be needed and, perhaps, even made a preliminary walk-through of the process and staging areas that will be required that day. All of this has been in preparation for cutting up each half of the carcass into smaller pieces and to do it as safely, quickly, and efficiently as possible.

As mentioned earlier, a chilled carcass is easier to cut up than a warm one. From a health standpoint, it is also safer because a cold carcass will inhibit, but not entirely exclude, bacterial growth more than a warm one.

Warm muscle/meat is more difficult to slice into even cuts, although it is not impossible. Warm muscle does not "set up" its fiber structure like cold muscle does. If you plan to cut up the carcass soon after you have split it in half, you can use a cold bath to cool it. Remember that you need to chill the carcass or cool the cuts you make as soon as possible.

You can create a staging area where you can place the half carcass for cutting while the other half is cooling. A sturdy table that is unlikely to collapse under the weight of the carcass is best. It should be cleaned and disinfected prior to placing any meat on it, and then washed with clean water and towel dried.

To begin, place one half of the carcass in a large tub of cold, clean water. Add ice over the top, and then, if not cutting up the other half, place it on top and add ice. If it is a warm carcass, you will likely need to add ice to replace that which melts as the heat is drawn from the muscle. Siphon off the water as you add ice to replace it. Try to keep the top half completely submerged at all times. It typically will float near the top because of the oxygen contained within the muscle, not unlike when you are swimming. You can use a clean, heavy weight placed on top if no one is available for keeping it under water.

At this point there will be little contamination of the meat because you have not cut into it. Yes, you cut down the backbone or spine to divide it in half, but if you made a straight centerline cut, you didn't expose any of the muscles—just the bones and spine. And unless you skinned it right away, the rest of the carcass and muscles should be covered with either the skin or the silverskin lining that lies between the skin and the muscles. This can be easily rinsed or cleaned prior to cutting into the muscles or making carcass divisions.

One more consideration about cooling the carcass: To properly chill it, you should maintain an ice water temperature between 34° and 38°F for a minimum of 24 hours. You may be able to work at it sooner if you have a refrigerator unit large enough to place the carcass in. If so, maintain a temperature of 38°F (at or near the bone) within twelve to twenty-four hours. You will need a reliable thermometer that can be inserted at the thickest muscle level in order to make sure all parts are sufficiently chilled. You should remove all the tissue heat before working on it.

A local meat market that also specializes in butchering may be able to help you if you can arrange chilling time with them. Whether you work with a local market or cool the carcass on your own, you can begin cutting it up once the temperature has stabilized.

CUTTING UP THE CARCASS

Before beginning to cut up the carcass, make sure your knives are sharp and that you have a clean and sanitary work surface, and pans or tubs in which to place the cuts for wrapping.

You will need a meat saw, not a wood-cutting saw, for cutting the larger bones. Be sure it is thoroughly washed with soap and hot water. Pay particular attention to cleaning the teeth on the blade and the fore and rear joints where the blade attaches to the handle. Your knives should be cleaned and hand or eye protection used. While it is not necessary to dress like a meat cutter, that, in fact, is what you are. You may want to consider using a hard-surface apron that can provide protection against accidental abdominal or leg stabbings if your knife slips. These are simple safety precautions that many have found useful.

Cutting up the carcass is not a complicated process, and you can easily accomplish it on your own or with the help of your family or friends. However, some simple techniques will help you produce a quality finished product.

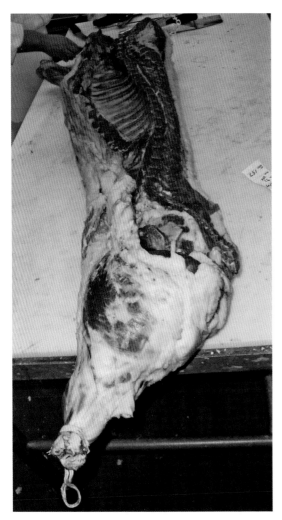

After the carcass has cooled to remove all the heat, you can begin to cut it up. Use your sturdy table to begin deconstruction. Make sure it has been thoroughly cleaned with hot, soapy water and towel dried.

BONE DUST

The first is to be aware of bone dust. You will need to use a meat saw to cut through large and small bones that your knife cannot split. A meat saw is often safer to use than a knife because of the bone density, shape, and position of the bone being cut. Bones are hard and most knives will not be able to slice through them.

Each time after you saw through one bone, be sure to wipe off the blade of any material embedded in the teeth or clinging to the blade. As you saw back and forth through a bone, it will create a mixture of meat and bone particles as the blade passes over the muscle and bone on each stroke. Clean off the blade with a separate, clean dry cloth, or rinse the blade each time with fresh, clean water. Also make sure the meat cut is cleaned if particles attach to it. Cleaning the blades and cuts will help eliminate any "crunchy" texture from the small bone chips and will reduce the area where bacteria can grow.

You can cut up a pig carcass in several different ways. The one described here is only one method, but it is a simple and reliable one. You may have ideas about other processes and those can be used as well. The only caution is that you do it efficiently, safely, and quickly. Begin by pulling the half carcass from the ice tub and place it on its exterior side on your table.

Use your scraper after each cut made with your saw to remove any bone particles.

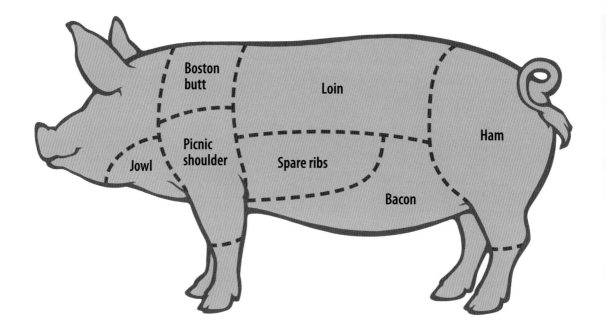

CUTTING STEPS

The guiding principle in cutting a carcass is that you will make as many cuts at joints that you can as it will then be easier to separate into smaller portions.

To begin, cut off the legs at the knees and the rear hocks with your meat saw. You can first cut through the skin with your knife and then use the saw to cut through the joints. Once through the bone, you can cut the skin on the lower side with your knife to completely sever it.

Don't spend time with these right now as they are not valuable parts of the pig. You have greater value cuts to work on. You will want to remove the hams next. By removing the large end, you will have an easier time cutting it into pieces.

Locate the aitchbone and the fifth lumbar vertebrae. Make your first cut with your meat saw at a point about 2½ inches in front of the aitchbone. Then make a saw cut between the fifth and sixth vertebrae. Stop cutting with the saw after severing the spine.

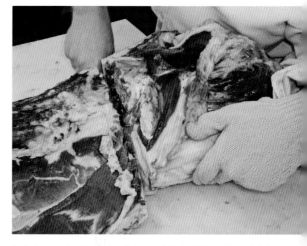

Begin by removing the rear leg. Make a cut in front of the aitchbone (pelvic bone) and between the fifth and sixth lumbar vertebrae with your saw. The pelvic bone will be part of the ham. Finish the cut with your knife.

Use your knife to complete the cut through the rest of the tissue. The pelvic bone will still be a part of the ham once you've separated it from the spine. Depending on your storage space,

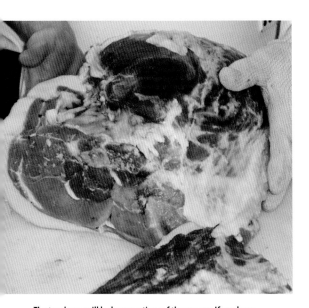

The two hams will be large sections of the carcass. If you leave either the skin on or a lot of fat, it will prevent them from drying out too quickly.

You can slice the bone out by removing the muscle around it. This will make smaller pieces to work with later and to either smoke, cook, or freeze.

this may be a concern because of its size. Or it may be too large a piece for convenient cooking, in which case you may want to trim out the large bone.

If you want to trim out the bone, start by slicing and following the bone from the pelvic end down to where the ham attaches to the point above the hock. Then carefully cut around the bone with your boning knife until the ham is free.

You can also make smaller bone-in ham steaks by cutting first across the ham with your knife, making a ½-inch to ¾-inch slice down to the bone, then cutting through the bone with your saw, and then finishing the cut with your knife. These ham steaks will be easier to wrap and package.

You can choose to trim most of the fat and skin off the ham before doing anything else with it. If you do, leave about ¼ inch on the outer surface to keep it from drying out too fast.

CUTTING THE SHOULDER

Next, you will want to saw off the shoulder at the third rib. To locate this rib, count them by beginning at the neck and counting toward the loin. At the third rib (on the side toward the rear end), make your cut through the spine and shoulder muscle. Again, first use your saw and then use a knife to cut the meat.

The shoulder has two primal cuts—the Boston butt and the picnic shoulder—and three minor cuts: the neck bones, jowl, and clear plate. It is easier to work with the shoulder if you cut it down into smaller pieces. This won't harm the cuts; it will simply give you more portions that will be easier to cook later.

After separating the shoulder from the carcass, you should remove the neck bones. There are seven neck vertebrae. You should trim these out as completely as possible, and they can be used for soup stocks or sauces, or maybe barbequed.

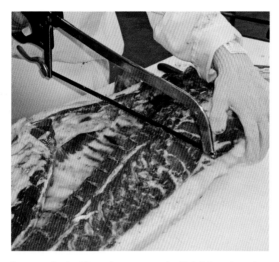

To remove the shoulder, make a saw cut at the third rib from the neck. This will include the Boston butt and picnic shoulder.

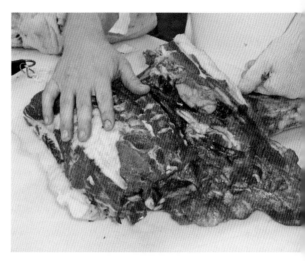

The shoulder will now include portions of the jowl, the clear plate at the top, and the foreshank of the upper front leg.

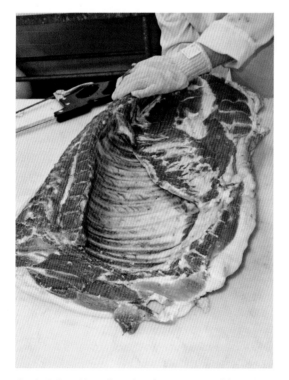

The ribs, belly, and loin will now form the center section of the remaining carcass to be cut into divisions.

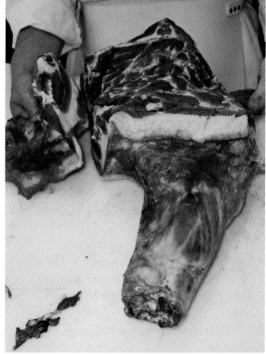

To remove the jowl, make a cut at the fat collar just above the shank and cut across the top of the shoulder.

Next, remove the jowl. Begin at the fat collar immediately above the foreshank and continue across the top portion of the shoulder. You should trim out as much muscle as possible. These pieces can be smoked or used for sausage.

At the very top of the shoulder is the clear plate. It contains mostly fat, such as the fatback. To remove it, trim close to the large meat portion just below it—the Boston butt. Trim out any lean meat and the rest can be rendered for lard.

To divide the shoulder into the Boston butt and picnic, locate a spot that is about 1 inch below the shoulder blade and parallel with the breast, and then make your cuts to separate them.

The Boston butt contains one shoulder blade. This is a popular cut, which can be removed as the pork shoulder blade steak.

You can square the picnic by sawing off the foreleg first. The picnic contains most of the shoulder bones, including the foreshank and the arm bones. The foreshank has a lot of connective tissue because these muscles power the front legs. The foreshank can be trimmed and then you can remove the arm bone.

This carcass side has now been squared up, more or less, with the removal of the front and rear legs. What is left is the main body of the carcass side.

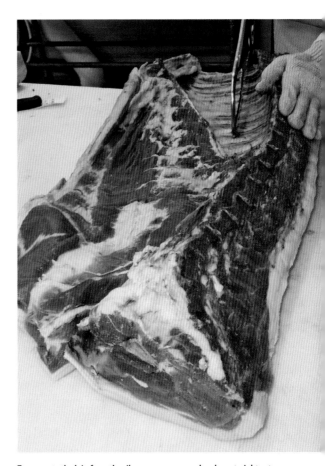

To separate the loin from the ribs, use your saw and make a straight cut across the ribs that runs parallel to the loin to a point just below the tenderloin muscle where the ham was cut off.

SEPARATE THE LOIN AND RIBS

Next, separate the loin from the ribs. You will want to make careful cuts on the loin to separate it because this is usually the most valuable cut in the carcass; it may be about 16 percent of the carcass weight.

Because of the pig's anatomical structure, the pork loin is a longer area than that of a beef or lamb loin. You should separate the loin from the shoulder by sawing across the third rib.

Then use your saw to separate the loin from the ribs. Make a straight cut that runs parallel to the loin. Start at a low point of the spine that was near the shoulder and saw across the ribs to a point just below the tenderloin muscle, where the ham was cut off. This cut may appear to be diagonal because of the shape of the spine and the ribs. This cut will then separate the loin from the spare ribs and belly. Set them aside as you work on the loin.

TRIMMING THE LOIN

You can trim much of the fat off the loin, but leave about ¼ inch of fat on it as this will be useful when cooking it.

The two ends of the pork loin include muscles from the leg or ham and the shoulder. There are divisions called the blade section, which is located nearest the shoulder: the center, that is most highly valued, and the sirloin section, nearest the rear leg or ham.

You will want to take care when cutting the loin so you do not slice into it. You can trim out the loin for boneless chops or loin roasts. Or you can leave the bones in and slice it into separate pork chops. We'll leave the bones in for this discussion.

Begin with the part of the loin that was nearest the shoulder. Make cuts between each rib bone and the attached cartilage to create blade chops until you reach the fifth rib.

The fifth to the tenth ribs are called the center-cut loin chops. These are the most desirable portions of the whole carcass because they contain the tenderloin. Cut these separately like the blade cuts.

The last section, or sirloin, is the most posterior portion of the loin and runs from the eleventh rib to the hipbone. These cuts are referred to as the sirloin chops, and they will contain portions of the eye and tenderloin, the top sirloin muscle, and hipbone.

BELLY AND SIDE

The last portion is the belly, or side. Because of the cut you just made to remove the loin, the

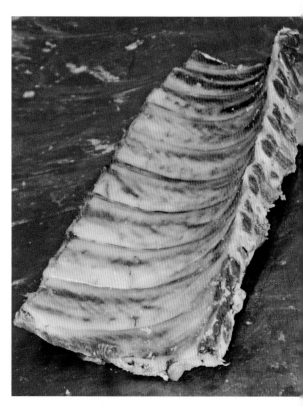

The belly or side is your last cut. Use a straight knife to closely slice the belly from the ribs. The resulting slab will be used later for cutting into bacon.

The spare ribs will be cut from the rib cage you just severed from the loin area. These can be sliced with your knife into sets of four to six ribs for grilling, roasting, braising, or broiling.

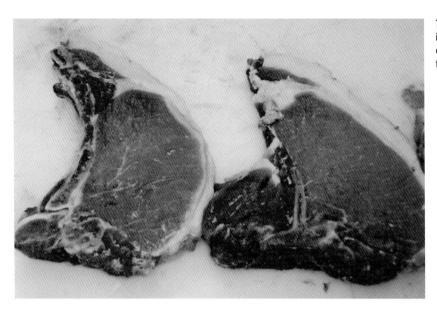

The loin can be cut into individual chops or it can be cut out as a single, separate piece for a loin roast.

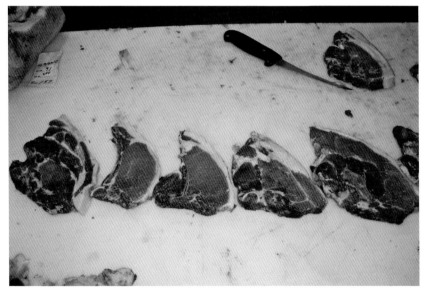

The cuts from the back or loin will vary in size and shape as you move from the front of the loin (far left) to the rear (far right). The most tender and valuable cuts are found in the middle.

lower parts of the ribs are still attached. These should be trimmed out. Use a straight knife to make cuts between the back fat and the belly to remove the ribs.

Depending on the type of cut you used to separate the loin, you may have different rib lengths, and this will also affect the width of the belly piece to some degree. There will be some remaining bones and cartilage with the spare ribs that should be trimmed out because you don't want this to become part of the bacon.

After you have removed the spare ribs, you can either slice the belly into strips for bacon to use or freeze, or you can smoke the entire side and cut it up later. You can square up the belly by trimming the edges evenly. This will also remove any rudimentary mammary glands and teat lines that may remain. Be sure to remove the outer skin layer, if you haven't already done so, before you slice strips or smoke it.

The spare ribs can be used fresh and barbequed, or cured and smoked. Spare ribs are generally cut into portions containing between two and six ribs for ease of storing or cooking.

HALFWAY THERE

You have now deconstructed one-half of the pig carcass. Using the same steps, begin with the other half, which should still be chilling.

If you have help with wrapping your cuts, you can proceed. If not, make sure you wrap the portions quickly and place them in a freezer. Fresh pork that has been properly chilled can last safely for 1 to 2 days in your refrigerator. After that, it should be frozen.

One note on food safety: **Do not** let any pork that has been chilled to warm to room temperature before it is frozen. This is inviting problems.

You can freeze pork immediately after cutting and wrapping. You can freeze it after it has been cooled in your refrigerator. But you **cannot** chill it, then let it warm up, and then freeze it.

If the pork cuts warm to room temperature or above 40ºF after having been cooled or chilled from 34º to 40ºF, you must cook them. Otherwise bacteria have an abundant opportunity to grow.

THE SKULL

The skull is comprised mostly of hard bone with a jaw and teeth. Cheek muscles work the jaw, which can be trimmed out and used in a variety of ways. The whole head can be roasted or boiled. Remove the tongue if you desire to use it separately.

To remove the tongue, place the top of the skull on the table to expose the underside of the jaw. The jawbone forms a V-line, and inside this is the tongue. Begin by making a deep arcing cut where the head was severed from one side of the jaw to the other. Then run the blade as close to the jawbone as you slice toward the front of the jaw. When you reach the front point of the jaw, withdraw your knife and make a second cut along the opposite side to the point of your previous cut. This should allow the tongue to be pulled free or cut free if there are still any attachments.

Trim the skin off the skull, and the side jaw muscles should now be exposed. Use your trimming knife to cut as close to the bone to remove the cheek and jaw muscles and then do the same for the other side.

EARS

The ears are considered a delicacy in some countries after they are fried. You can remove them by making a deep circular cut around each ear. They will need to be stripped of all hair and skin before you use them.

SNOUT AND EYES

The snout can be used in the same way as the ears, although this is mostly cartilage that moves because of very small muscles. Try to remove what you can if you want to use it. The eyes have little or no real nutritional value. You can let your chickens have a go with them.

BRAINS

The pig brain is more difficult to get at because of the hard skull bone. Pigs are not considered ruminants and therefore are not susceptible to bovine spongiform encephalopathy (BSE), as cattle are. No naturally occurring cases of this have been identified in the pig; however, it has been produced experimentally by direct inoculation of infected bovine brain tissue into a pig's brain. Feeding infected brain tissue, however, has not resulted in any disease.

Although the current evidence suggests that pigs cannot transmit BSE like cattle, or chronic wasting disease (CWD) like deer, moose, or elk, you should be cautious about consuming any soft tissue such as brains. Having raised your own pig to butcher, you are fully aware of what it was fed. You also have observed its behavior daily, and if there are no indications or suspicions that it was in any way an unhealthy animal, then your risk of eating the brains is likely to be very minimal. In the end, the choice is yours.

While there is some protein content that may be derived from eating the brains, it is not the recommendation of this book that they be used for your family. They can, however, be safely fed to pets in one form or another.

Queen Elizabeth II views a pig at an agricultural show.

Chapter 5
USING PORK BYPRODUCTS

Many portions of a pig's carcass can be utilized. However, not every part of their body is made of choice cuts such as chops or hams. All parts of the pig that are not included in the various cuts are called *byproducts*. These include the skin, bones, hair, teeth, fat, brains, nonconnective tissue, tendons, and internal organs.

This chapter will focus on using the edible byproducts such as the liver, heart, tongue, kidneys, blood, and intestines that may find uses in your meals in one form or another. These byproducts are sometimes referred to as *variety meats*, and you may develop a taste for a particular part with some experimentation and guidance. Maybe you already enjoy them as most byproducts can be included in specialized dishes or ground up for sausage making.

Several of these byproducts, such as the liver, heart, and kidneys, are high in protein content and, by themselves, highly nutritious. Some people with health conditions such as Creutzfeldt-Jakob find organ meats, such as liver, tongue, and heart, to be helpful in their diets. The variety meats are generally more perishable than other meats and require quick cooling or cooking after harvest if not frozen.

It is mainly our unfamiliarity with these parts that tend to make them off-putting to many families. However, these variety meats can be utilized in specialized dishes, or many can be ground up for use in sausages.

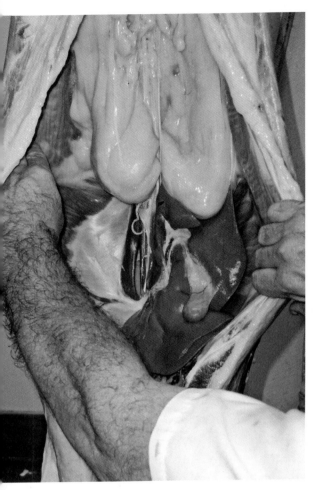

The internal organs will appear like this when the carcass is suspended and opened. The white intestines are at the top. The spleen can be seen next to the liver on the right. Study a pig anatomical chart before you begin butchering to familiarize yourself with the organ positions.

Byproduct	How to Cook or Use
Liver	Fried, braised, sautéed, broiled
Heart	Roasted, stuffed, in sausage
Tongue	Braised, boiled, pickled, fried
Kidneys	Broiled, in sausage
Brains	Broiled, braised, fried, in sausage
Lungs	Broiled, roasted, fried, braised, in sausage
Spleen	Roasted, braised, in pâté
Bones/ Marrow	Roasted, used for soup stock
Blood	In sausage, black pudding
Tail and Ears	Roasted, grilled, broiled, pickled, braised, deep-fried
Feet	Roasted, grilled, deep-fried, braised
Intestines	Roasted, braised, deep-fried
Snout/Lips	Roasted, in soup stock, pan-fried
Skin	Roasted, fried, braised
Lard	As cooking fat, in baking
Jowl	Roasted, braised, fried, in sausage
Uterus	Roasted, broiled, sautéed, curried, stir-fried
Bladder	As a pouch for stuffing
Testicles (male pig)	Roasted, fried, broiled, in sausage

LIVER

The liver lies near the stomach and is held in place by connective tissues that surround it. Remove as much of this tissue as you can and then slice the liver into ⅛- to ¼-inch strips. Then freeze it after wrapping. Large pieces of liver can also be frozen whole. Because the liver can be about 2 percent of the carcass weight, it is generally too large to freeze as one whole piece.

Liver can be fried, braised, sautéed, or broiled. It can also be ground or chopped for use in sausages, loaves, spreads, or it can be used in combination with other dishes.

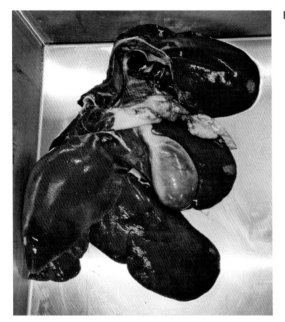

Examine the liver and remove the spleen. Cool them as quickly as possible.

HEART

The heart should be sliced halfway open for inspection and to allow any residual blood to drain out. Like the liver, you should trim off any connective tissue and chill the heart quickly after removal from the carcass.

The heart can be cooked with moist heat or roasted like a turkey. It can be stuffed with dressing or pepper and stitched shut for cooking. The heart is generally less tender than the liver, although it can have an excellent flavor. It can also be chopped or ground up for use in sausages.

Examine the heart and slice it in half to allow any residual blood to escape and to help it cool.

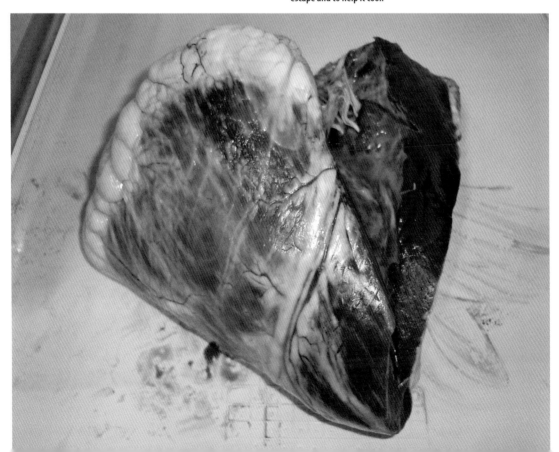

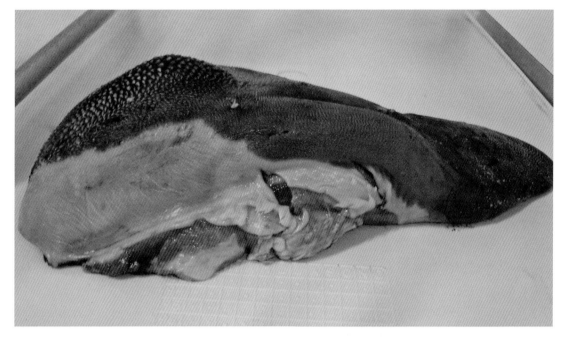

The tongue should be removed and trimmed of any muscle roots. Cool it as soon as possible.

TONGUE

The pig tongue can be used for cold meat sandwiches after braising and cooling and being thinly sliced. The tongue has a tough outer membrane that must be removed before eating. This can be done by blanching, followed by moist heat cooking for an extended time. Once this membrane is trimmed, the rest can be cooled and sliced.

KIDNEYS

The kidneys of a pig may be broiled and skewered and are more tender than those found in beef animals. They can be included in meat casseroles, stews, and other dishes. They can also be ground or chopped for use in sausages.

The kidneys will be surrounded with fat. This should be removed so you can examine their color and firmness, and to cool them more quickly.

PIG'S BRAIN

At the time of this writing, no scientific evidence is available indicating that eating the brains from pigs is detrimental to your health or can produce a food-borne illness. In fact, they can be found in specialty markets and are used in other countries such as China and Korea as a stir-fry staple. Pig brains differ from ruminants such as cattle in that they do not carry the prions identified as precursors of bovine spongiform encephalopathy (BSE) or any variant of Creutzfeldt-Jakob disease. So, go ahead if you choose and try dishes made from the brain of the pig you raised and butchered. You know what it ate and how it lived and should have confidence that it will be healthful.

LUNGS

Pig lungs are used in many countries for eating with a wide variety of preparations. About forty-five years ago, the US Wholesome Meat Act declared pig lungs unfit for human consumption. They have since made a comeback of sorts among enthusiasts devoted to exotic animal parts. Lungs contain about as much protein as a beefsteak but with less fat. Europeans have no qualms about using this part of the pig, and since you have a fresh supply handy, you may want to experiment with yours. You can eat them solely as a dish by themselves, perhaps with garnishes, or ground up for inclusion in sausage making.

The lungs (upper right) should have a pinkish color. All the internal organs should have bright colors, which indicate a healthy pig.

HEAD

The pig's head can be used for a specialty dish roasted whole, or it can be trimmed of all meat, fat, and skin and the skull used for a flavorful soup stock once the brains, eyes, ears, snout, and tongue have been removed because it will contain a good quantity of gelatin. To make use of any marrow in the head, it will need to be crushed to open the hard bones and expose the marrow to the liquid medium used. If using the head for roasting, you will need to remove all hair by scraping, singeing over an open pit or barbeque grill, plucking, shaving with a disposable razor, or using a gas torch. If singeing, be sure to do it in open air as the flame may pose a fire hazard inside your house or apartment, and the smell of burning hair may be overwhelming. Once the hair is removed, you should scrub the head vigorously with a stiff brush and then coat it with lots of salt, rubbing it into the skin.

SPLEEN

The pig's spleen can be used for a specialty dish or processed into a pâté. The spleen will appear deep reddish in color when ground up and may be mixed with ground beef to alter the color and taste. The spleen's function is like a lymph node that cleans the body of old red blood cells and antibody-coated bacteria. In texture, it is more like liver than any other organ. The spleen is high in iron, niacin, phosphorus, selenium, vitamins B12 and C, and zinc. One downside is that it is very high in cholesterol, and a 3-ounce portion can contain up to 145 percent of your daily cholesterol requirement. The spleen can be stuffed, braised, roasted, or ground finely and made into a pâté. They can remain fresh for 2 to 3 days, or frozen and used later, but within 3 months.

BONES AND MARROW

You will likely have a lot of bones left over from your butchering process. Many will be contained in meat cuts that you freeze or use right away. Those that are left over from trimming off the meat can still be useful to you, particularly the marrow. The marrow is the inside of the bones and is found in red and yellow varieties. Red marrow produces red blood cells, while yellow consists of mostly fat. Marrow is a good source of protein and is high in monounsaturated fats, which help decrease bad cholesterol levels. Bones can be roasted or boiled for their soup stock components. You won't be eating the bones themselves. Rather, you will be enjoying the marrow as it cooks out. Your dogs can enjoy the bones after you have finished with them.

BLOOD

Blood represents about 5 percent of the pig's market-weight carcass. A 200-pound pig will have about 10 pounds of blood in its body. However, only about 3.5 percent on average can be harvested because the rest remains in the tissues. If you've butchered a 200-pound pig, then you will have about 7 pounds of blood to use. How do you use this much blood? It can be made into such things as blood sausage, black pudding, blood pancakes, or in a Filipino soup called dinuguan that uses pig's blood twice; it's mixed in with the broth and appears again in a blood-sausage form.

One disadvantage of having this amount of blood to use at one time is that it needs to be used immediately or shortly after it is harvested. Or it has to be treated in some manner so that it doesn't coagulate into a firm mass. Under normal circumstances, blood will begin to thicken and clot when exposed to air. This coagulation process will turn the liquid into a gelatinous cake, ready to be used in many recipes and preparations. To keep blood fluid, the coagulation process must be halted. This can be done by using an acid, usually vinegar, in a ratio of one part vinegar to five parts blood. While blood starts as a sterile liquid as it leaves the animal's body, it is such a nutritious liquid that it is an ideal environment for pathogens or spoilage microorganisms. This will require you to use it immediately, in an altered or diluted form within 1 to 2 days, or freeze it.

To claim the blood from your pig as it's draining, you will need to stir it frequently and add about 5 percent salt to stabilize it. It must be used within 1 to 2 days and should be cold when it is mixed with other ingredients. Before use, it must be stirred and filtered, such as through a cheesecloth. Otherwise, it may clump together with your other ingredients. Don't process it any later than the second day. If your refrigerator is capable of maintaining temperatures of 33ºF, the blood may keep for 2 to 4 days. Even if you add salt or nitrite, they will not be effective in extending blood's shelf life.

No fewer than thirty dishes worldwide use blood in the cookery in one form or another. Only one is included here—black pudding—while blood sausage is included in the sausage section of this book. You are encouraged to look deeper into the uses of blood in creating unique meals if so inclined. Black pudding has long been a staple of Irish and British households while blood sausage has a long worldwide history.

Okay, what about the rest of the blood that's not used right away? One of the best ways is to freeze it and keep it below 32°F until ready for use. However, in time, blood plasma separates from the blood and water accumulates on top and the blood must be stirred before use. Freezing it

with vinegar, at a ratio of 1 cup vinegar to 6 cups blood, is a safe way to prolong its freshness.

If all else fails and no one wants to contend with the blood, you can mix it in water and apply as a fertilizer to your garden plants.

A PIG TAIL AND EARS
A pig's tail is full of bones while the ears are mostly made of cartilage. The pig's tail is cooked in a variety of ways, including roasting, grilling, broiling, pickling, or braising. Or a tail can be deep-fat fried until crispy and then eaten like bacon. Pig tails contain a nice balance of lean and fat and can be breaded for roasting. They also can be used in soups and stews.

The ears of your pig are considered a delicacy in some countries when fried or sautéed and eaten as crispy treats. Like the tail, you should remove the hair on the skin before using. After they are cleaned of hair and thoroughly washed, the tail and ears can be stored in a refrigerator for about 1 week. They can be frozen for up to 3 months with few resulting quality problems. If you freeze them, be sure to wrap them well to avoid freezer burn.

ROASTED PIG TAIL
The tail can be cooked like ribs. It can be baked by wrapping it in tinfoil until done and then uncovered to crisp it. Add a barbeque sauce and pig tails can mimic spareribs. The only problem is that your pig has only one tail. If you want more, you will need to go to a local butcher market to source more. One pig tail will make a treat but will not make a meal.

PIG'S FEET
You will get four feet from your pig, and like the tail, they may not be a sufficient quantity for a

meal by themselves. You can source more pig feet from a local butcher market to supplement what you need. Pig's feet are sometimes referred to as trotters. These assemblages of skin, bones, fat, and connective tissue are a good source of flavor. They can be prepared and used in a variety of ways, and while they do not have any significant amount of muscle to them, they do yield a mellow pork flavor and a large amount of fat and gelatin that can be infused into many other dishes. They can be grilled, roasted, deep-fried, or braised with satisfactory results. If you braise them for a long time, the skin can be removed from the bones and pressed together, breaded and fried, or stuffed with fillings.

Pig's feet can be frozen to last for a long time without losing quality. If not frozen, they should be used within 2 days while being kept cold in your refrigerator. Just like using other pig parts, the feet should first be thoroughly cleaned and all hair removed before freezing.

PIG INTESTINES

Pig intestines are sometimes also referred to as *chitterlings*. These are the large intestines of the pig and will have a pungent smell. They will need intensive cleaning because they can cause illness if not cleaned well because this is the fecal passageway of the pig. Healthy intestines should have a pinkish-beige color to them. They can be sautéed, deep-fried, roasted, or braised. The alternative to eating them is to clean them and use them for sausage making. Either way, you will first need to make sure the bacteria are killed.

First, boil them for 5 minutes prior to cleaning them to kill the bacteria. This will not change the taste and will help to clean them as you will loosen the particles and any fat attached to the inside.

After boiling, remove them and place in cold water. Rinse three or four times, changing the water after the second rinse.

PIG SNOUT AND LIPS

The pig's snout includes the ridge above and below the nostrils, and the circular cartilaginous plate. It can weigh as much as 1 pound and contains some meat located on the back side of the plate. These are the muscles that control the snout's movement and are surrounded with fat. The snout and muscles can be trimmed out with a boning knife and used for soups. After the soup has been cooked, the snout can be removed from the pot and pan-fried and eaten as a crispy treat. Their texture will have a rubbery, slightly crunchy feel and can be used in stir-fries as well.

PORK SKIN

The skin of the pig is often called the pork rind, and when fried or roasted, it is typically referred to as pork scratchings or pork cracklings. The rind is sometimes used in sausage making to help improve consistency. The tough skin of a pig can be made edible by a two-step process of rendering and drying it, and then frying what's left.

Pork skin is processed differently in countries around the world and is often a popular snack. The more tasteful varieties come from a combination of roasting or frying and adding salt to the outer layer. Since the fat has been removed through the cooking process, it provides a crunchy sensation. One advantage of this process is that the skin can be sliced into sections and frozen and later retrieved and processed without altering its flavor. Any rancidity will be limited because the fat that causes this condition is removed. Dried or frozen pork skin can be rehydrated in water and flavoring can be added before frying. Cooking makes the rinds expand and float to the oil surface. They can then be removed from the fat, flavored, and air dried.

Pork rinds processed this way will be very tasty but, unfortunately, will also be high in fat and sodium content. They are low in carbohydrates and can be considered an alternate snack. However, they are higher in protein and contain less fat than the typical potato chip. Almost half of the pork rind's fat is unsaturated, mostly oleic acid, putting it the same class as olive oil. No matter how you justify their consumption, pork scratching will still be a high caloric snack. Yet it is a good way to use the skin of your pig without having to throw it away. Even if you don't want to consume all of your pork rinds, your dog may find their crunchy texture very enjoyable.

PORK LARD

Lard from pigs was a kitchen staple for generations of rural and urban households. It was plentiful and easy to procure, it was reasonably priced for those who had to purchase it, it had a good shelf life, and it helped make the best piecrusts and biscuits imaginable.

Society fashions evolve, and eventually lard acquired a stigma that it was an artery-clogging, heart attack–inducing fat that consumers, cooks, and bakers should steer clear of. Despite the hysteria created against lard, it is a naturally rendered fat product that does not contain the preservatives used in today's commercially produced hydrogenated forms.

Lard contains monounsaturated fat in the form of oleic fatty acid, which is very healthy and great to use in almost any recipe that calls for fats. It is an excellent fat to use for deep-frying, baking,

and pan cooking. Some of the best lard can be produced from your pig.

All animals contain fats within their bodies. As you deconstruct your pig carcass, you will find multiple regions of it with significant amounts of fat. Don't throw it out or feed it to your chickens without first considering rendering it. With a little guidance, you can have your own supply that can last many months.

A pig has two basic types of fat: leaf fat and back fat. Leaf fat is from the interior of the animal near the kidneys, and back fat is from the long centerline of the pig's back, which, because the animal is a quadruped, is located at the very top of the pig's skeletal structure, between the loin and the skin.

Pig fat may vary a little in color depending on its location. Back fat may have a reddish color to it because of the muscle structure close to it while leaf fat will most likely be purely white in color. Both are usable and back fat may have a richer flavor.

As you are trimming the carcass, dedicate a clean, separate container or tub where you can place the fat pieces. You can work with the fat after you finish with the more valuable meat cuts. But be sure to cool it off and not let it get too warm. Since the four factors instrumental in making fat rancid are light, moisture, air, and warmth, all lard you process should be kept in a dark, cool, dry place.

Pork fat is considered a soft fat, especially when compared to beef fat. It is typically 40 percent saturated fat, 50 percent monounsaturated fat, and 10 percent polyunsaturated fat. Pasture-raised pigs that consume a diet supplemented with grain have a lower percentage of polyunsaturated fat, which is a good thing to consider. The reason lard is so good for cooking and baking is that the percentage of its saturated fats protects the more vulnerable mono- or polyunsaturated fats from oxidizing with heat. Research shows that oxidized fats—when the double bonds in mono- or polyunsaturated fats break—can create free radicals in the human body. An excessive amount of free radicals can lead to poorer health and inflammation of muscles, joints, and blood vessels. Lard can be part of a healthy diet.

One intriguing aspect of using lard is that it is flavor neutral, meaning, if properly processed, it will not impart a pork flavor to the dish, such as with coconut oil, which can. Although lard will pick up the dishes' flavor, you are eating that specific dish anyway, so lard becomes an adjunct to the flavors already there.

After cod liver oil, lard is the second-highest food source of vitamin D. One tablespoon of lard contains 1,000 IUs of vitamin D, which helps with calcium absorption for healthy bones and teeth. But the vitamin D produced by pigs only comes from those that have access to sunlight, such as pasture-raised, outdoor pigs, and not those in confinement. Pigs store the vitamin D in their fatty tissues, which can then be transferred to lard.

PIG'S JOWL

A pig's jowl refers to the two side cheeks of its head, below the eyes and the underside of the jaw in front of the throat. It is sometimes referred to as jowl bacon because the cheek muscles are layered with fat. However, it has a higher meat-to-fat ratio than bacon from the belly. Belly bacon has a 1:3 ratio of meat-to-fat, while jowl bacon has a 2:1 meat-to-fat ratio. This means jowl bacon may be cooked a bit differently than traditional bacon.

After you have trimmed the cheeks off the head and sliced the skin off, you will have two slabs of meat and fat. These can be smoked and cured, or sliced into thin strips for cooking. These can also be used as a binding ingredient in pork liver sausages such as liverwurst and Braunschweiger. After being cured, fried, or smoked, this meat can be chopped into small pieces and used as a garnish, such as bacon bits on salads.

To use the fresh jowl from your pig's carcass, begin by trimming the cheeks off the side of the head. Begin below one ear and score a line toward the snout, cutting under the eye. When you reach the snout, slice back toward the neck joint along the jawbone until you've made an oval cut.

Next, trim close to the bone to remove the cheek. Use the same method for the other side. Then trim the outer skin off the two pieces.

To fry the jowl, cut the pieces into ¼-inch-thick strips like traditional bacon and place in a hot skillet. There will be enough fat that you won't need to add cooking oil. Fry the slices on one side until brown and crisp. Flip each over and allow the other side to cook. Monitor and turn the slices every 2 minutes to evenly cook them while they brown and crisp. Remove them when finished.

Baking pig jowl can achieve the same result as frying it. Set your oven to 400°F. Place the strips in a baking or roasting pan, or on a rimmed baking sheet that is lined with parchment paper. This will prevent the strips from sticking to it. Arrange the strips so they do not touch each other and season with salt and pepper, as desired.

Place the sheet in the oven and roast for 20 minutes. Check for doneness after 15 minutes and turn them over, but continue to bake until crispy. The strips should have a dark brown color and most of the fat should be rendered out.

Remove the sheet from the oven and place the strips on clean paper towels. Pat off any fat on the strips. Carefully pour the rendered fat from the sheet into a heat-resistant bowl. It can be strained, and after it cools, it can be poured in a glass jar and used as lard.

While the roasted strips are cooling, you can sprinkle them with salt, pepper, sugar, or a variety of seasonings to suit your tastes.

PIG UTERUS

While likely not everyone's choice of a pork dish, the pig's uterus (providing it is a female pig that was butchered) can be used. The reproductive tract of a young, nonpregnant female will be found anterior to the vulva and forms a long V-shaped tubular structure.

It can be curried, roasted, broiled, sautéed, or used in stir-fry dishes. It will not be a large amount to work with, and although it is technically a muscle composed of smooth muscle cells, it is also considered an organ. It is made up of three layers: the inner lining, the middle layer (which makes up most of the uterus volume), and an outer lining. This thickness gives it the density to be sliced into pieces.

The uterus should first be placed in a salt brine for about 24 hours. Then rinse it thoroughly with cold, clean water. Remove the attached ovaries and discard. Slice the tubes along their length to open them up, or slice across to make rolls about 1 inch in length. Be adventurous and devise recipes of your own or use one for a stir-fry.

PIG BLADDER

You can use the pig bladder, not so much to be eaten, but, rather, as a pouch in which to stuff other meats to be cooked. It can be likened to a porcine version of haggis.

The bladder should be rinsed in a salt bath for 12 hours and thoroughly cleaned. You can then stuff it with chicken or turkey, vegetables, and bread stuffing soaked with red wine.

TESTICLES

If you raised a male pig that still has intact testicles, you can use them. For the best flavor, they should be grilled so that the smoke imparts a flavor that will enhance the gamey undertone of the glands. Grilling allows the testicles to maintain their form, but they can also be sliced and grilled. You need to first remove the outer membrane and then slice them in ¼-inch-thick pieces. They can also be chopped and ground up for sausages, fried, or broiled.

Chapter 6

PRESERVING YOUR PORK

Butchering a pig likely will yield more meat than your family can eat quickly while it is still fresh. This means you will need to have a plan to preserve the rest to keep it useable later on. Different preservation methods serve different purposes. Those discussed here are different from smoking and curing, which will be addressed in a separate chapter.

Although meat preservation is one of the later stages in the whole butchering process, it is one that needs your initial attention and planning. Before you even begin to lay a hand on your live pig, you need to know where you will store the extra meat so it doesn't go to waste. As you learned earlier, you will have little time to delay preserving the meat safely.

This chapter will lead you through several methods that can be used to examine the choices and/or alternatives that you have to safely preserve the meat for future use.

Different preservation methods serve different purposes, but all are used to inhibit bacterial or microbial growth. You can freeze, can, dry, salt, or pickle your pork. These are the major forms of preservation that offer the safest long-term storage options. Large commercial applications such as vacuum packaging, irradiation, sugaring, and using lye, modified atmosphere, and high pressure are being used to preserve pork, but these are industrial-scale methods that will not be discussed here.

You should plan to use as much of your pig's carcass as possible. That's why you raised it and it is the ethical thing to do.

Freezing is one of the most commonly used preservative methods and has several advantages. It is a fast, simple way to stop microbial growth. One advantage of freezing is that the meat does not deteriorate through freezing, although some quality and texture can be affected by long-term storage, commonly called freezer burn.

Canning is most often done with sealed glass jars or metal cans (which will not be discussed here). It involves cooking the pork to a boiling point for a specified time as a form of sterilization. The sealed jars containing meat pieces are submerged in boiling water or placed in a pressure cooker. One advantage of canning is that you can have a ready-to-heat meal after the jar is opened. It can serve as a backup in case of a freezer unit malfunction, and it provides another option if you encounter insufficient freezer space.

Drying, besides cooking, is the oldest method of food preservation and involves dehydration of the meat. Removing the moisture inside the muscle tissue significantly reduces the water activity to prevent, inhibit, or delay bacterial growth. By reducing the amount of water in the tissue, you also reduce the weight of the meat, which can help with storage space.

Salting is used to cure meats by drawing moisture out of the tissue through a process of osmosis. Salt or sugar can be used separately or in combination.

Pickling is the use of a brine, vinegar, or any spicy edible solution that is used to inhibit microbial action because most bacteria cannot survive in an acidic environment.

FREEZING

Freezing remains one of the best preservation methods you can use after processing your pig carcass. It provides for long-term storage without destroying vitamins or the pork's nutritional value. Freezing the pork almost completely inactivates the enzymes and inhibits the growth of spoilage organisms.

It is important to always remember that your pork meat temperature must be brought down to 40°F within 8 hours (preferably less) to prevent growth of spoilage microorganisms that lie deep within the carcass tissues. If the meat has not been cooked and is going directly to a freezer, it must reach a temperature of 0°F within 72 hours to prevent the growth of putrefying bacteria.

The cuts you make to be frozen should be similar in size and thickness, or individually wrapped and ready for cooking. Try not to wrap large portions that need deconstruction later. You can have large portions, but plan to use them together. Do not refreeze any pork that has been thawed to make into smaller pieces. You will need to cook all the pork that has been thawed. Besides, packaging smaller cuts will allow them to freeze more quickly and more evenly than very large pieces or chunks. Always attempt to minimize the number of times the meat needs to be handled and exposed to surfaces after it has been thawed.

CANNING

After freezing, canning is the most commonly used preservation method for long-term pork storage. Canning usually takes two forms:

sterilized and pasteurized. Sterilized pork does not need refrigeration and can sit on shelves for extended periods as long as the container remains intact. Pasteurized pork will require refrigeration to inhibit spoilage.

Using appropriate procedures to can pork will ensure quality and safe storage. Canned pork can be preserved by hermetically sealing the jar, which prevents air from escaping or entering it. By applying heat to the scalded pork, you destroy the microorganisms that are capable of producing spoilage. Using proper sanitation during the breakdown of the pig carcass will help minimize the number of organisms that may be present at canning time.

Canning involves a time-temperature relationship in destroying most microorganisms. A specific internal temperature must be reached and held for a minimum amount of time to destroy the microorganisms present. This method is most often applied to destroy the spores that can lead to botulism.

These temperatures and times are at the high end of any other methods. A safe cook, which is considered one that destroys the botulism organisms, requires a minimum of 3 minutes

Glass Canning Jar Tips

- The jars come in several sizes, although pints are most popular.

- They require covers or lids that can be firmly tightened.

- Rubber rings and metal lids with a sealing gasket can be used.

- New rings and seal lids must be used each time for new canning.

- Discard used lids or rings.

at 250ºF. Achieving this sterilizing temperature will require the use of a pressure cooker. These typically operate under pressure of 12 to 15 pounds per square inch. Pressure changes the boiling point of water and allows it to rise above the normal boiling point of 212ºF.

Canning pork to sterilize it has its advantages. Probably the greatest advantage is the long storage life over a wide temperature range. Canned pork that is properly done can last several years and still be edible, although some flavor deterioration may occur.

The two most important principles of canning are providing sufficient heat and creating a perfect seal of the container. Only the best and freshest pork should be used because canning only preserves the meat; it does not improve the quality of it.

Glass jars are typically used in a method called hot pack. This involves packing the meat into the jars and processing the jars in boiling water or steam. The advantages of this method are that the jars are completely sealed and the meat has no further exposure to outside influences or organisms.

PRESSURE COOKERS

Many types of pressure cookers are commercially available, such as stovetop and electric models. Most models are made of aluminum or enameled steel. Whichever model you choose, the same principles apply. It should be substantially constructed and should have a pressure indicator, a safety valve, and a petcock or vent.

To begin canning, thoroughly wash each glass jar in hot, soapy water and rinse it in clear, hot water. The jars can air dry by placing them on clean towels. Inspect each jar and test the cooker before you begin. Examine the jars and lids for cracks or nicks. Run your finger over the top lip of each jar. If you detect any imperfection, any chip,

or any crack, *do not* use then for canning because they may fail during the heating process.

If the jars appear intact, you should fit a new ring to each jar, partly fill them with hot water, and adjust the lid and seal. Invert each jar and watch for leakage or small bubbles rising through the water as it cools. If you notice any bubbles, then there is an imperfect seal. This means you should check again and discard the lid, ring, or jar, depending from where the bubbles originate. You can also test the rubber rings by doubling them over. If you find any cracks, discard them.

FILLING WITH PORK

To fill the jars with pork, first add cubed pieces of pork from the shoulder, Boston butt, jowl, hocks, feet, or other parts you wish to use. Do not tightly pack down the pieces into the jar. Then follow these steps:

- Fill each jar with clean water to within 1 inch of the rim.

- Place a small amount of water in the bottom of the cooker. (The water level should reach the bottom of the rack, which keeps the glass off the chamber base and allows the water and steam to completely surround the jars.)

- Place the jars on the rack inside the cooker.

- Place the jars so they do not touch each other.

- Adjust the lid of the cooker and fasten tightly so no steam can escape through the petcock.

The petcock should stay open until steam has poured out steadily for 10 minutes or more.

Then close it to allow the pressure to rise to the level directed in the owner's manual, usually 10 pounds.

BEGIN PROCESSING

To begin the canning process, add the pork-filled jars to the cooker and clamp on the airtight lid. The cooker is then set over heat or heat is applied electrically. As the water temperature rises, it creates pressure inside the cooker. This raises the temperature higher than that what is used in ordinary stove cooking and cooks the meat more quickly. Pressure cookers have a gauge on the lid that will show the number of pounds of pressure, indicating the temperature.

When the appropriate pressure is reached, you should adjust the heat to keep the same pressure without variation. For pork, process it for 3 minutes at 250°F before removing the heat. After the processing time is completed, the heat should be removed and the cooker left idle until the pressure drops to 0.

A safety valve releases pressure after the cooking is completed, and the petcock provides an outlet for steam to escape. This will lower the pressure inside the cooker. When the temperature and pressure are completely reduced to 0, open the petcock to release any remaining steam. After all the pressure inside is released, it will be the same as the ambient pressure in your kitchen and this will allow you to open the lid without any problems. Having pressure still inside the cooker that is higher than room temperature may cause the lid to fly off as it is loosened or hot steam to escape out the top, which may cause injury. *Always* allow the steam to fully escape from the cooker via the safety valve or petcock prior to loosening the handles that secure the lid to the cooker or attempting to remove the cover. Do not let the cooker sit unopened for any length of time after the steam is down. This may create a vacuum inside the chamber and make it very difficult to open the lid. If this happens, reheat the cooker for a few minutes until the lid loosens.

After cooling, remove the lid and check the jars. They will be extremely hot, so be careful with handling them. A jar tweezers to lift them from the inside will help protect you from the hot glass. Use oven gloves to avoid steam burns on your hands. You may have to hand-tighten any loose rims, but make sure the lids are completely sealed before you do. If any jar is imperfectly sealed, such as the lid lifts off the glass rim, use the meat soon. It is safe to eat because it has been cooked. But you *cannot* save any such jar for later use; recycle it.

The jars should not be reopened and refilled under any circumstances. Once they are sealed and cooked, leave them to cool and use later. Place the jars on a rack or towel to cool, but keep them away from cool drafts. Some canners turn the jars upside down as they cool to check for any leaks or bubbles, which indicate a poor seal.

After drying, label the jars with the canning date. After 10 days, recheck the jars. Immediately discard any that exhibit cloudiness or signs of spoilage. Do not eat their contents under any circumstances and do not feed the meat to your pets.

DRYING AND SALTING

Drying is probably the oldest method of food preservation and involves dehydrating the meat. The removal of water from the pork significantly reduces the water activity to prevent, inhibit, or delay bacterial growth. Reducing the amount of water in the pork also reduces its total weight and can make it easier for transport.

Simply drying the meat is not really sufficient in today's food climate to provide a safe, shelf-stable product. While dehydration may be able to be used for short-term storage, it is not a long-term solution unless the meat has been sufficiently cooked and dried. That will reduce the quality and create a jerkylike texture. Because this is not a recommended preservation method, it will not be discussed here.

Salting, however, can be a useful form of pork preservation. Salting cures pork by drawing moisture out of the tissue through a process of osmosis. If salting is used, it requires a high concentration of salt, which may be a health concern for some. Because salting typically requires concentrations of up to 20 percent to kill most species of unwanted bacteria, this method is not being discussed here.

PICKLING

Using a brine, vinegar, or any other spice-based edible solution to cure pork is commonly referred to as pickling. Pickling can involve two different forms: chemical pickling, which uses a brine solution, or fermentation pickling, which is often used with vegetables, such as making sauerkraut.

The edible liquid used in chemical pickling typically includes agents such as a high salt brine, vinegar, alcohol, and vegetable oils, particularly olive oil. The purpose is to saturate the food being preserved with the agent. This may be enhanced in some cases with heating or boiling. Some foods that can be chemically pickled include pork hocks and feet, peppers, eggs, and fish. Fermentation pickling is generally not used with meat but can be used with foods that offer a good compliment to meat during a meal.

WRAPPING

Rancidity is the bad taste or smell derived from fats or oils that have spoiled. It develops differently in animal carcasses, depending on their fats' ability to absorb oxygen from the air. Rancidity can affect the taste, odor, and palatability of the fat and adjoining tissue. Different animal species produce different fats. Pork fat is high in unsaturated fatty acids, which have the ability to absorb oxygen, resulting in a possible shorter storage life. You can reduce oxidation effects by eliminating air exposure to the pork. One good way for home use is to properly apply a wrapping material that is airtight and moisture proof.

Wrapping, or containing pork in airtight units, serves several purposes. It forms a barrier between the meat and oxygen present, reducing oxidation; it prevents odors present in the refrigerator transferring from one food to another; and it helps in preventing cross-contamination between pork and other foods that may occur through drippings or splashing. Outside the refrigerator, wrapped or covered pork cuts are less exposed to flies, insects, or pets.

Also, wrapping or enclosing pork cuts in containers will help keep them fresh rather than left uncovered while sitting on a refrigerator shelf. Uncovered meat has more exposure to oxygen, which can cause bacteria to multiply faster. Oxygen also dries out the meat surface much quicker.

You can use several products to wrap, cover, and store your pork cuts, including aluminum foil, plastic wrap, resealable plastic bags, airtight containers, freezer paper, waxed paper, and parchment paper. While each has their advantage, using proper meat wrapping paper for your pork cuts is still the best option.

Freezer paper is a plastic-coated paper designed for wrapping foods intended to be stored in a freezer. It is much heavier material than aluminum foil or plastic wrap and provides good protection for storing pork cuts. You can also write on it so that you know what is inside without having to open it.

Waxed paper is a moisture-proof material that is made by applying wax to the paper surface. It is often used as a preparatory step on which to lay foods prior to cooking or baking. It has a slightly higher heat tolerance than plastic wrap but should not be used in cooking or baking. Its nonstick surface properties make it a good barrier between frozen pork cuts wrapped in the same package.

BRINES

A brine is a salty liquid used for preserving food for long-term storage. It is salt with water, but when the two combine, they create a powerful solution. Salt is a great preservative and, when in a water solution, it will penetrate meat faster than if rubbed on. Brines add flavor, and when spices or other aromatic substances such as garlic, onion, or peppers are added, they will also infuse the meat by osmosis as the salt works its way inward.

Brines can have a powerful effect upon the pork, so you will need to use them carefully. You can use too much salt and brine for too long a period. As with other spices you may use, it is often best to underuse salt when making pork products.

One of the best ratios to use for a brine is 1 cup salt per 1 gallon water. If there is a concern about salt intake in your diet, you can reduce the salt and sugar in your brine, but remember that only a small portion of the salt actually enters the meat.

Simple Rules for Brines

- Never reuse a brine when finished. Always discard it.
- Observe recommended brine times.
- Chill the brine thoroughly before adding the pork.
- Allow the pork to rest in the refrigerator after brining. This disperses the salt more evenly within the tissues and allows the exterior to dry.
- Always brine pork in the refrigerator.
- Brine well ahead of cooking to allow it to rest.

SIMPLE ALL-PURPOSE BRINE RECIPE

1 gallon nonchlorinated water

1 cup pickling salt

½ cup sugar

Seasonings of choice

Mix all ingredients in a large pot or kettle and bring to a simmer. Stir the liquid until the salt and sugar are completely dissolved. Remove from heat and allow to cool to room temperature. Refrigerate until chilled.

Typical Pork Brine Times

Pork Chops, 1½ inches thick, 2 hours
Boneless Pork Loin, 4 pounds, 12 hours

HAM STORAGE CHART

Type of Ham	Refrigerate	Freeze
Fresh (uncured) ham, uncooked	3 to 5 days	6 months
Fresh (uncured) ham, cooked	3 to 4 days	3 to 4 months
Cured ham, cook-before-eating; uncooked	5 to 7 days or "use-by date"*	3 to 4 months
Cured ham, cook before eating; after consumer cooks it	3 to 5 days	1 to 2 months
Cooked ham, vacuum sealed at plant, undated; unopened	2 weeks	1 to 2 months
Cooked ham, vacuum sealed at plant, dated; unopened	"Use-by" date*	1 to 2 months
Cooked ham, vacuum sealed at plant, undated or dated; opened	3 to 5 days	1 to 2 months
Cooked ham, whole, store wrapped	7 days	1 to 2 months
Cooked ham, half, store wrapped	3 to 5 days	1 to 2 months
Cooked ham, slices, store wrapped	3 to 5 days	1 to 2 months
Spiral-cut hams and leftovers from consumer-cooked hams	3 to 5 days	1 to 2 months

HAM STORAGE CHART

Type of Ham	Refrigerate	Freeze
Country ham, uncooked, cut**	2 to 3 months	1 month
Country ham, cooked	7 days	1 month
Canned ham, labeled "Keep Refrigerated," unopened	6 to 9 months	Do not freeze
Canned ham, labeled "Keep Refrigerated," opened	7 days	1 to 2 months
Canned ham, shelf stable, opened***	3 to 4 days	1 to 2 months
Lunchmeat ham, sealed at plant, unopened	2 weeks or "use-by" date*	1 to 2 months
Lunchmeat ham, sealed at plant, after opening	3 to 5 days	1 to 2 months
Lunchmeat ham, sliced in store	3 to 5 days	1 to 2 months
Prosciutto, Parma, or Serrano ham, dry Italian or Spanish type, cut	2 to 3 months	1 month

  * Each company determines its "use-by" date and stands by it.

 ** A whole, uncut country ham can be stored safely at room temperature for up to 1 year. The ham is safe after 1 year, but the quality may suffer.

*** An unopened, shelf-stable, canned ham may be stored at room temperature for 2 years.

Note: Freezer storage is for quality only. Frozen hams remain safe indefinitely.
Source: USDA Food Safety and Inspection Service, 2015

Chapter 7
MAKING SAUSAGE AND BACON

Sausage making has a long history that extends back over 3,500 years. By using various parts of your pig, you will join that long line of artists who created safe, edible, nutritious, and tasty sausages.

This chapter will explain many of the different varieties of sausages that can be made with pork and lead you to explore new food avenues. Aside from sausages, which have many specialties, you will learn how bacon can fit into breakfast, lunch, or dinner menus, or even as snacks.

As with other foods, certain principles need to be observed and incorporated into your practical methods so you can produce a satisfactory end product. You may learn to use spices you've never considered before to make distinctive-flavored sausages. And you may learn the cross-cultural aspects of producing traditional sausages often identified with other countries.

Before we get into the procedures and sausage-making dynamics, let's take a look at the variety of sausages that you can make at home. While numerous sausages can be made from different animals, fowl, and wild game, we will concentrate on those that use pork as their main ingredient. Most sausages will contain some amount of pork in them, even if it is only the fat.

The trimmings of fat and meat can be used in sausage making. You may have as much as 25 pounds to work with.

The US Department of Agriculture (USDA) only classifies sausages in this country as two types: uncooked, which includes fresh bulk sausage, patties, links, and some specialty smoked sausages; and ready-to-eat, such as dry, semidry, and cooked.

Like other fresh meat, fresh sausages are highly perishable and must be refrigerated or frozen until ready to be cooked, and they must be cooked before eating them to avoid health risks. Ready-to-eat sausages have been processed and preserved with salt and spices and may be dried or smoked. These types of sausages, which can include sausage sticks, can be eaten out of hand, or cooked and heated, such as hot dogs.

INGREDIENTS, ADDITIVES, AND SPICES

The ingredients, additives, and spices you add, and their quality, will greatly affect the taste and texture of your final sausage products.

An ingredient is a component of a recipe that is added in a specific quantity. For sausage making, they may be raw meat and nonmeat materials.

The interaction between the ingredients and meat materials used will determine the different flavors and textures between sausages.

You will control the ingredients and spices that you add to your sausage. By understanding the properties of each, you will be able to create products that meet your requirements and tastes, whether it is to limit the preservatives you eat or to avoid high-fat products routinely available at retail markets.

You should keep one simple rule in mind when creating your sausages, regardless of which kind they are: your finished product is only as good as the ingredients it contains. The pork you start with should be fresh, have a proper lean-to-fat ratio, and exhibit good binding qualities. Clean pork that has been cut in sanitary conditions is a prime requirement. The pork used should not have been contaminated with bacteria or other microorganisms at any stage of processing or cutting.

INGREDIENTS

Most of the ingredients you will use are readily available for purchase at local supermarkets or meat markets, or from other specialized commercial businesses. Licensed retail outlets that specialize in such products are another source. Internet businesses that sell ingredients for meat processing can provide them for sausage making. If buying ingredients from businesses outside your area, be sure to check their licenses and ask about the sources they access for their products. Always check their labels to be sure you know what you are adding to your meat.

The main ingredients for your sausage making are likely to be based on meat derived from pork, beef, and perhaps veal—either separately or in combination. Other ingredients may include hearts, tongues, livers, kidneys, and stomachs. Generally, those cuts with the lowest economic value are used for sausage making.

Nonmeat ingredients are used to provide flavor, inhibit bacterial growth, and increase the amount of sausage produced. These may include water, salt, sugar, nonfat dry milk, soy products, extenders and binders, spices, and cures.

BINDERS AND EXTENDERS

Binders refer to the ability of the meat ingredients to hold and entrap fat and water, and for the lean meat particles to be held or bound together. Extenders are used in some products to increase the moisture content and texture rather than to stretch the amount of product derived from a certain volume of meat available.

- Water and ice are added sometimes to add moisture and keep the sausage cold during processing. Cold temperatures delay bacteria growth and add to the final product quality. Water also helps dissolve salts for better distribution within the meat.

- Salt serves three functions in the meat: preservation, flavor enhancement, and it draws out protein to help bind the mixture.

- Sodium nitrate and nitrite are used for curing meat as they inhibit growth of a number of pathogens and bacteria that cause spoilage, including those that cause botulism, the lethal food poisoning. Nitrate and nitrite are the most regulated and controversial of all the sausage ingredients. It is strongly recommended that a commercial premixed cure be used when nitrate and/or nitrite is called for in the mixture.

- Sugar is used for flavor and to counter the taste of salt. It helps reduce the pH in

meat because of the fermentation of the lactic acid.

- Ascorbates and erythorbates are Vitamin C derivatives that speed the curing reaction. They can be used interchangeably in cured sausages to which nitrite has been added.

- Milk protein–derived extenders, including nonfat dry milk, dried whey, and buttermilk solids, are used widely in processed meat products. They are added to improve binding qualities, flavor, and slicing characteristics. They are used in such products as bologna and frankfurters (hot dogs) to stabilize the emulsion.

SPICES, SEASONINGS, AND FLAVORINGS

Many different spices, seasonings, and flavorings are used in sausage production to increase taste. For home sausage making, they are generally added by personal preference and taste or to follow general guidelines for a particular recipe. By combining different levels of various spices, you can create unique and distinctive sausages.

Spices, seasonings, and flavorings typically are not included to add to the nutritional value of the sausage, although they provide some minute traces of nutrition. Spices vary greatly in composition and may be added as whole seeds, coarsely ground, or in powdered form. Some of the major spices used include the following:

- **Allspice:** A reddish-brown pimento berry available whole or ground. Pungent, clovelike odor and taste. Used in bologna, pork sausage, frankfurters, hamburgers, potato sausage, headcheese, and other meat products.

- **Basil:** Marketed as small bits of green leaves, whole or ground. Aromatic, mildly pungent odor and used in dry sausage such as pepperoni.

- **Bay leaves:** Elliptical leaves marketed whole or ground. Fragrant, sweetly aromatic with slightly bitter taste. Used in pickling spice for corned beef, beef, lamb, and pork tongues and pigs' feet.

- **Caraway seed:** Curved, tapered, brown seeds sold whole. Slightly sharp taste.

- **Cardamom seed:** Small, reddish-brown seeds sold whole or ground. Pleasant, fragrant odor; used in bologna and frankfurters.

- **Cloves:** Reddish brown sold whole or ground. Strong, pungent, sweet odor and taste. Used in bologna, frankfurters, headcheese, liver sausage, corned beef, and pastrami. Whole cloves can be inserted into hams and other meats during cooking.

- **Coriander seed:** Yellowish-brown, nearly globular seeds sold whole or ground. Lemonlike taste. Used in frankfurters, bologna, knackwurst, Polish sausage, and other cooked sausages.

- **Cumin seed:** Yellowish-brown oval seeds sold whole or ground. Strong, somewhat bitter taste used in chorizo and other Mexican and Italian sausages, and used in making curry powder.

- **Dill seed:** Light-brown oval seeds sold whole or ground. Warm, clean, aromatic odor used in headcheese, souse, jellied tongue loaf, and similar products.

- **Garlic, dried:** White color ranging in forms of powdered, granulated, ground, minced, chopped, and sliced. Strong odor with pungent taste.

- **Ginger:** Irregularly shaped pieces, brownish to buff-colored sold whole, ground, or cracked. Pungent, spicy-sweet odor but clean, hot taste. Used in pork sausage, frankfurters, knackwurst, and other cooked sausages.

- **Mace:** Flat, brittle pieces of lacy, yellow-to brownish-orange material sold whole or ground. Somewhat stronger than nutmeg in odor and flavor. Used in bologna, mortadella, bratwurst, bockwurst, and other fresh and cooked sausages.

- **Marjoram:** Marketed as small pieces of grayish-green leaves either whole or ground. Warm, aromatic, slightly bitter and used in Braunschweiger, liverwurst, headcheese, and Polish sausage.

- **Mustard seed:** Tiny, smooth, yellowish or reddish-brown seeds sold whole or ground. Used in bologna, frankfurters, salamis, and summer sausages.

- **Nutmeg:** Large, brown, ovular seeds sold whole or ground. Sweet taste and odor; used in frankfurters, knackwurst, minced ham sausages, liver sausage, and headcheese.

- **Onion, dried:** Similar to garlic in forms available. Used in luncheon loaves, Braunschweiger, liver sausage, and headcheese.

- **Oregano:** Marketed as small pieces of green leaves, whole or ground. Strong, pleasant odor and taste. Used in most Mexican and Spanish sausages, fresh Italian sausage, and sometimes in frankfurters and bologna.

- **Paprika:** Powder form ranging in color from bright red to brick red. Slightly sweet odor and taste. Used in frankfurters, fresh Italian sausage, bologna, and other cooked and smoked sausage products.

- **Pepper:** Black, red, white in color and sold whole or ground. Penetrating odor and taste, ranging from mild to intensely pungent. Black pepper is the most used of all spices, but white is substituted when black specks are not wanted, such as in pork sausage and deviled ham. Red pepper is used in chorizo, smoked country sausage, Italian sausage, pepperoni, and fresh pork sausages.

- **Rosemary:** Needlelike green leaves available whole or ground. Fresh, aromatic odor, somewhat like sage in taste.

- **Sage:** Grayish-green leaves sold whole, ground, or cut. Highly aromatic with strong, slightly bitter taste. Used in pork, pizza, and breakfast sausages.

- **Savory:** Sold as dried bits of greenish brown leaves. Fragrant, aromatic odor and used primarily in pork sausage.

- **Thyme:** Marketed as bits from gray to greenish-brown leaves, whole or ground. Fragrant odor with pungent taste used in pork sausage, liver sausage, headcheese, and bockwurst.

HERBS

Whether they are added by volume or weight, herbs and spices are a very small percentage of any sausage but have an enormous influence on the character and flavor of the end product. In either case, the best herbs and spices are those that are purchased fresh or homegrown, and used soon after harvesting. If you purchase either or both, try to buy new products rather than older ones because new vintages will have retained their potency more than older ones. Store herbs and spices in a cool, dry area away from heat and light (two elements that have a significant impact on freshness). Fresh herbs and spices rarely retain their optimum flavors longer than 6 months.

SALT AND PEPPER

Salt and pepper add flavor and aroma to sausages. Many different types of salt are available, but those without additives, such as iodine, provide maximum flavor. Pepper can be purchased as whole peppercorn and ground when needed. Recipes may make distinctions between three forms of pepper: finely ground, medium grind, and coarse grind. Finely ground is a fine powder with no large pieces in it. Medium grind refers to flakes that will pass through a typical shaker. Coarse grind has small bits that may be ground in either a pepper grinder with a coarse setting or with a mortar and pestle.

CASINGS

It is not necessary to stuff fresh sausage meat into a casing. It can be left in bulk form or made into patties. But if ground into bulk form, it will have to be used within 1 or 2 days to retain its freshness and quality. Most sausages are made by inserting the ground ingredients into some forming material that gives them shape and size, and it holds the meat together for cooking and smoking, or both. This material is called a casing.

Two types of casings are used in sausage making: natural, and manufactured or synthetic. Although their purposes are the same, their origin is very different.

Natural sausage casings are made from parts of the alimentary canal of various animals that can include the intestinal tracts from pigs, cows, or sheep. One advantage for using them is that they are made up largely of collagen, a fibrous protein, whose unique characteristic is variable permeability. This allows smoke and heat to penetrate during the curing process but without contributing undesirable flavors to the meat. Natural casings can be purchased from companies that offer sausage-making products or they can come from the pig you are butchering. Packing houses that save casings will flush them with water and pack them in salt before selling them to casing processors. The casing processor does the final cleaning, scraping, sorting, grading, and salting before you purchase them. If using your own animal casings, it is important they are thoroughly flushed and cleaned, and placed in a salt brine prior to use.

CLEANING CASINGS FOR HOME USE

You can clean your own pig casings for sausage production after they are removed from the body cavity. Because they are unlikely to be the first parts you work with from the carcass, they need to be set in cold water to reduce their temperature to prevent spoilage. If working alone, the cold-water tub should be set up prior to beginning. If working with others, you can designate another to handle this part. Several things need to be considered if using the intestines for meat casings. The first is sanitation. The intestines will likely be filled with excrement, which contains the E. coli bacteria and needs to be kept away from any organs that you plan to use later. If you plan to use several or all of the organs attached within the viscera, you will need to cut them away from the mass of intestines and stomach prior to placing them into the cold water to reduce the chances of contamination. Cut the heart, liver, spleen, kidneys, or any other organs away from the intestines and stomach, and place them aside in a clean, cool container. Making a cut at the point where the stomach and large intestines meet should then separate the stomach and intestines.

If you have used a cord or string to tie off the end of the intestine at the anus when you made your cuts to remove it, then one end should still be tied. After making your cut at the stomach and intestine junction, place that end in an empty pail or other container and allow the intestinal materials to drop into it. Depending on the size of the animal you butchered, there may be much intestine to work with or relatively little. You may have to use your hand to strip as much of the excreta out of the intestine as possible. When finished, you can place the intestines in a cold-water bath that has been primed with salt and work with them later, after finishing working with the more valuable meat cuts of the carcass.

Intestines make very good natural casings for your sausages because they are largely collagen and will easily break down during the curing process, yet still are strong enough to hold the meat during the stuffing process. Their flexibility makes them an attractive alternative to synthetic casings. But good casings are also clean casings and you will need to prep them for use by removing all of the excrement and intestinal linings before using them.

To begin properly cleaning your casings, you will need to invert the intestine by turning it inside out. After removing any cord or string that has closed one end, start by turning one end of the intestine inside out to create a lip,

Natural sausage casings can be made from the pig's intestines. Remove them from the stomach before cleaning them.

much as you would roll down your socks, except that you are not making a rolled-up mass. You want to pass the rest of the intestine through this roll as if you were peeling a banana without breaking it. When the inside of the intestine has completely become the outside, you should thoroughly wash it in a cold 0.5 percent chlorine solution. Use a soft-bristle brush to very gently scrub the excess fat, connective tissue, and any residual foreign or fecal materials off it. Although the intestine can withstand some good scrubbing, you need to be careful not to overdo it or you may leave little tears in the membrane that can rupture and break during the stuffing process.

After thoroughly cleaning the intestines, rinse it with clean, cold water and invert it back to its original form. Use a salt solution (1 teaspoon of salt per gallon of water) for storage overnight. If you are not using the casings for several days, they can be kept in this solution with cold temperatures. If not using them for 2 weeks or longer, you can put them in a freezer suspended in this salt-saturated solution. This solution will also inhibit the growth of bacteria that thrive on salt as well as other bacteria that may have

Clean the intestines by removing as much of the fecal material as possible by stripping them. Then run water through to flush them out. Place in a salt brine and soak before giving them a more thorough cleaning.

five classes: bungs, middles, smalls, stomachs, and bladders. Bungs and middles are best used for dry sausage; smalls for fresh sausage such as chorizos, bratwurst, bockwurst, and Polish; stomachs for headcheese; and bladders for minced luncheon meats. Small hog casings, from the small intestine, are probably the most widely used and easiest to find at a local meat shop if you run out of your own.

MANUFACTURED AND ARTIFICIAL CASINGS

The alternative to natural casings is a group of manufactured or artificial casings that are made from edible or inedible materials. Fibrous casings are popular because they are uniform in size and easy to use. They are made from a special paper pulp mixed with cellulose and are inedible and must be peeled away before eating. However, they provide the most strength of any casing available. Three of the most common types of synthetic casings include collagen, cellulose, and artificial.

Some natural casings are called collagen casings and were developed to be an edible casing replacement for natural casings, and to

survived the chlorine solution bath. Before using your stored casings, gently flush them in lukewarm water to remove any clinging salt. They are then ready for use.

Hog casings have a wide variety of use and are considered to be an all-purpose casing. They have

Small links, hot dogs, or small sausages can be made with the smaller size intestine casings. These are smoked and cooked for safe eating.

have the uniformity of a manufactured product. They are made from the gelatinous substances found in animal connective tissue, bones, and cartilage, and are mechanically formed into casings. Because of their lower structural strength, these casings generally are made into small-diameter products and are ideal for breakfast links, or fresh, smoked, and dried sausages. Unlike large cellulose and fibrous casings, collagen casings should not be soaked in water before use. They are easier to work with when dry.

Cellulose casings are made from cotton linters, the fuzz from cottonseeds, which are dissolved and re-formed into casings. Cellulose casings are crimped into short strands and an 8-inch length may stuff as much as 100 feet of sausage. Small cellulose casings work well for skinless wieners and other small-diameter skinless products.

Artificial casings are frequently made from plastic and are inedible. They can be used for sausages cooked in water or steam, such as bologna and Braunschweiger.

If you are not using your own casings, you can purchase any of the manufactured or artificial casings from meatpacking companies, sausage supply businesses, local butcher shops, or, perhaps, through ethnic markets.

EQUIPMENT

You only need a few pieces of equipment to make sausage in your home. The three most important pieces include a meat grinder, a sausage stuffer, and a thermometer. Other pieces that you may find useful include a mixing tub, a scale, and a smoker if you want to do your own meat smoking and preservation. Sausage-making equipment is usually available from meat equipment supply companies.

MEAT GRINDERS

A meat grinder is used to reduce the size of the meat pieces into a pliable mixture. They can be operated by hand or electricity. Some food processors can do a good job of chopping meat, and some heavy-duty mixers may have a grinding attachment that will work.

Hand grinders have been used for generations and usually have several different size grinding plates or chopping disks ranging from fine, with holes ⅛ inch in diameter, to coarse, with holes ⅜ inch in diameter. All hand grinders will have a screw augur that is attached to the outside handle. A disc cap screws over the top of the grinding plate, holding it in place while the meat is forced through the holes by the augur. It is a simple process once you have it set up. Hand grinders typically have a tightening screw at their base so that they can be mounted to a table or sturdy support frame.

If you are doing small amounts of sausage, a hand grinder should be sufficient. Some large grinders make use of a small motor with belt attached. This is a fast, efficient way to grind a very large amount of meat in a very short time.

Food processors can be useful in producing finely ground or emulsified sausages, such as frankfurters, bologna, and some loaf products.

Remember that regardless of the type of grinder you use, it must be thoroughly cleaned with hot, soapy water before each use and between different batches.

SAUSAGE STUFFERS

You should consider buying a sausage stuffer if you plan on making your own sausages. Several types are available, including hand, push, crank, and hydraulic operated by air or water. They can be made of plastic, stainless steel, or cast iron. Many small meat grinders are capable of supporting a small stuffing horn.

The piston-type stuffer is one of the most common for home use. It is operated by air or water pressure and will press the sausage quickly into the casing, producing fewer air pockets than hand-operated, screw-style stuffers.

Depending on the amount of sausage you plan to make, you may need a large stuffing unit with different funnels for different casings. You can use a jerky extruding gun if you only want to make small sausage links.

A push stuffer is quick to reload but has a small capacity. With this type of stuffer, you manually push down on a handle to force the meat into the casing.

A crank stuffer has more capacity than a push stuffer and takes less effort to press the sausage into the casing because of the pressure created by your combined arm and screw action.

An extruder can be used to stuff casings, and several types will work well. Be sure it is thoroughly cleaned between batches that you make.

SAUSAGE FUNNELS OR HORNS

The sausage funnel or horn constricts the movement of the sausage from the meat tub into the casing. As the casing fills, it pushes itself away from the funnel as it elongates. The size of the funnel is directly related to the size of the casing. Funnels are straight tubes, not tapered, and may range from 4 to 6 inches in length. To decrease the possibility of tearing the casing, first coat the funnel with water or grease to help slip the casing over it.

OTHER EQUIPMENT

You should keep other items on hand during your sausage processing. Three important and useful pieces include measuring instruments—a scale, measuring cups, and thermometer(s).

Scales

For weighing meats and other ingredients, a reliable scale is essential. A scale that measures both in pounds and ounces should be sufficient for most of your needs. For recipes or curing chemicals where weights are measured in grams or ounces, a smaller scale may be necessary. If curing ingredients are being used, particularly sodium nitrite, it is very important to use a scale that can measure to the nearest one-tenth of a gram.

Measuring Cups and Spoons

Measuring cups and spoons, ranging from ¼ teaspoon up to 1 tablespoon, and ¼ cup to 1 cup for liquids or dry measure, will be useful for adhering to specific recipes.

Thermometers

Thermometers are essential to help monitor and maintain appropriate temperatures during the processing and cooking of sausages. Several types are available, including instant-read and oven thermometers. An instant-read thermometer is a probe containing two different metal coils bonded together. The coil is connected to the temperature indicator that expands when heated, moving the dial.

The sausage casing is slipped over the funnel at the start. Tie the end off tightly and press the meat into the casing.

Use an accurate digital scale for mixing any cures or other ingredients that call for small amounts, especially if listed as weight instead of volume.

As the casing fills, make twists at intervals to separate into small units. After these are smoked, they can be separated at the twists for easy use.

Instant-read thermometers are used to assess when a specific temperature has been reached to assure safe eating and in making smoked sausage. They are good for use in sausage making because they can measure the temperature of a food within 15 to 20 seconds. Although they are not used during the cooking process, they can be used at or near the end of it to check the final temperature. This will allow you to monitor the cooking progress without overcooking the product. Insert the probe about 2 inches into the center of the meat to ensure a safe, accurate reading.

An oven thermometer can be set on one of the racks to monitor the temperature within the oven during the cooking time. One disadvantage may be if you do not have a window to view the thermometer, you may have to open the door to check the temperature, allowing heat to escape and prolonging the estimated cooking time.

Always sanitize thermometers before each use and when moving from one meat to another to avoid cross-contamination. They can be washed in hot, soapy water, then rinsed and dried.

CALIBRATION

Regardless of the type of thermometer used, make certain the calibration is correct to achieve accurate cooking temperatures. You should calibrate thermometers before first use or whenever they are dropped. They are sensitive and can lose calibration from extensive use or when going from one temperature extreme to another. Inaccurate thermometers will give incorrect cooking temperatures and can be responsible for under or overcooked foods. Undercooked foods can pose health risks.

Two different methods can be used to calibrate thermometers: ice water and boiling water.

Ice Water Method

- Fill a 1-quart measure with crushed ice and water and stir well.

- Let sit 4 to 5 minutes to provide an environment of 32°F.

- Completely submerge the sensing area of stem or probe, but keep it from touching sides or bottom of container.

- Hold for 30 seconds or until dial stops moving.

- If the thermometer is not within plus or minus 2 degrees of 32°F, adjust accordingly. The ice water method permits calibration within 0.1°F. Some digital stemmed thermometers have a reset button, which can be pushed.

- Repeat process with each thermometer to be used.

Boiling Point Method

- Fill a pot with distilled water and bring to rolling boil.

- Insert the thermometer to completely submerge the stem or probe sensing area without touching sides or bottom.

- Hold for 30 seconds or until the dial stops moving.

- If the thermometer is not within plus or minus 2 degrees of 212°F, adjust until it does. The boiling point method permits calibration to within 1.0°F. Some digital stemmed thermometers have a reset button, which can be pushed.

- Repeat process with each thermometer to be used.

The boiling point of water is about 1°F lower for every 550 feet above sea level. If you are in high-altitude areas, adjust the temperature by calibration. One example is if you were at 550 feet above sea level, the boiling point of water would be 211ºF.

Any food thermometer that cannot be calibrated still can be used by checking it for accuracy using either method. You can take into consideration any inaccuracies and make adjustments by adding or subtracting the differences, although this is not a recommendation of this book. The thermometer that is inaccurate should be replaced to provide greater assurance of accurate cooking temperatures.

HOMEMADE BACON

Bacon is not only great tasting as a stand-alone pork product, but it also can be a versatile ingredient in many dishes. Most bacon is purchased in markets as strips. You can make these too, but because you have the belly section from your pig's carcass, you now have more options for it.

Certainly you can cut the belly slabs into strips, but you can also cut it into bigger pieces or chunks for stews, soups, and vegetable dishes. You can roast belly sections whole or grill them. Making bacon at home is not a complicated process. You can do it with a smoker, oven, or grill.

The belly is composed of fat and thin layers of muscle. The fat, by itself, has no real taste until it starts to break down during the heating process. The muscle tissue has cell membranes that contain fatty acids that disintegrate during cooking. These yield flavorful compounds, including aldehydes, furans, and ketones that contain molecules having distinct tastes or smells. Furans yield a sweet, nutty, caramel-like flavor. Aldehydes are identified with a green, grassy tone, and ketones tend to be buttery. Also, the breed of the pig will have an effect on this composition as well. The genetic characteristics inherent with a particular breed, such as Berkshire, produce exquisite flavors from their meat and fat than other breeds. Even if fed the same ration, two pigs from different breeds can yield different flavors, and this is largely influenced by genetics.

While these different flavor-influencing molecules are separate from each other, they exude a unique sensory of taste when adding smoke and the sodium nitrite found in the cure, and adding heat by frying it. You then create the mouth-watering tastes and aroma that is commonly associated with bacon.

Besides all of this, you will be creating bacon from an animal you have raised and not one from a large commercial pig farm. Because your pig has received a varied diet of pasture, grains, and an outdoor atmosphere rather than confinement, you will quickly notice the flavor difference when compared to bacon purchased in a supermarket. But then, that's one of the reasons you raised your pig in the first place.

Salt pork is another product cut from the belly or side. However, it is not bacon. It is salted and much fatter than bacon, but it is not smoked.

MAKING BACON

You need two things to make good bacon: a pork belly, and a cure or pink salt. There are two kinds of bacon: fresh, and cured and smoked. Fresh bacon has a mild flavor and is the simplest to make by following these steps:

- Coat the slab of belly with the basic dry cure previously mentioned.

- Cover and refrigerate for 7 days depending on thickness. Less if thinner, more if thicker.

- Remove from refrigerator at end of time and rinse with nonchlorinated water.

- Pat dry.

- Slice to preference, and then fry or cook.

CURING AND SMOKING BACON

Cured and smoked bacon is what you typically purchase at a food market. Once it is cured, it is hot-smoked to a temperature of 150°F, then cooled and sliced. Most bacon of this type is smoked in a smoking unit. However, you can roast the cured bacon in oven heat to that temperature in about 2 hours. It may not have the same flavor as smoked bacon, but the texture will be similar, especially after frying.

You can also grill a fresh belly slab over indirect heat, very slowly if you can properly control a constant and consistent temperature. This can then be used in a variety of dishes, or cut into smaller pieces for stews, roasted, or grilled whole.

After cooking, you can store it in your refrigerator for up to 2 weeks (see bacon storage chart at end of this chapter). Or, you can wrap it tightly with freezer paper and store it in your freezer for 2 months or longer.

Your options for making bacon infused with different cures are many. To make a sweeter bacon, you can add more sugar-concentrated products, such as maple syrup. To create a savory bacon, you can add ground garlic cloves, bay leaves, ground black pepper, nutmeg, and a host of other spices. Adding these to the cure won't inhibit the cure's action in the meat. So the options you have will be limited by your imagination as long as you adhere to the basic curing procedures and amounts required to produce a safe food product.

The steps to create a good bacon product include the following:

- First, trim the belly into squared or rectangle shapes that have neat edges.

- Spread the cure on a large baking sheet so the slab can be completely covered with cure as you roll it over. Cover with a thick, uniform coating.

- Place the slab in nonmetallic container that allows it to disperse liquid as it cures but still allows the belly slab to remain in contact with it. (Water will leach from pork by the salt for continuous curing.)

- Refrigerate the belly for 7 days, turning over the slab every 2 days.

- After 7 days, check for firmness. If it's firm, it is ready. If it's squishy, continue to refrigerate until firm.

- Remove the belly from the cure. Rinse thoroughly with nonchlorinated water, and it pat dry.

- Preheat the oven to 200°F.

- Place the slab in roasting pan or rack for cooking. Roast until the internal temperature reaches 150°F, about 2 hours.

- Remove the rind or skin while the fat is hot.

- Cool the bacon to room temperature.

- Once cooked, wrap tightly and refrigerate until ready to use (refer to the bacon storage chart at end of this chapter).

SMOKING BACON

To smoke the bacon slab that you have just cured, follow these steps if you have a smoking unit. Always refer to the manufacturer's directions and recommendations for the particular unit you have, but these are standard steps you can use:

- Preheat your smoker to 175°F.

HOME STORAGE OF BACON PRODUCTS

Product	Pantry	Refrigerator 40°F or below	Freezer 0°F or below
Salt pork	Not applicable (N/A)	1 month	4 to 6 months
Bacon	N/A	7 days	4 months
Canadian bacon, sliced	N/A	7 days	4 months
Dry-cured sliced bacon	10 days without refrigeration	4 weeks in refrigerator	3 months
Dry-cured slab bacon	3 weeks without refrigeration	4 to 6 weeks in refrigerator	3 months
Bacon cured without nitrites	N/A	3 weeks in refrigerator	6 months
Leftover cooked bacon, cooked by consumer	N/A	4 to 5 days	1 month
Cooked bacon, purchased shelf stable	Unopened in pantry (stored below 85°F) until the "use-by" date on the package	After opening, refrigerate and use within 5 to 14 days.	See product recommendations on package for specifics.
Cooked bacon, purchased refrigerated	Observe manufacturer's "use-by" date	Observe manufacturer's "use-by" date	3 months for best quality
Canned bacon in pantry	2 to 5 years	3 to 4 days after opening	2 to 3 months after opening
Bacon bits, made with real bacon	Unopened in pantry, good until "sell-by" date	After opening, refrigerate up to 6 weeks	1 to 2 months
Imitation bacon bits, made with soy	4 months in pantry	Refer to jar for refrigerator storage	Not necessary for safety

Source: USDA Food Safety and Inspection Service, 2013

- Place the bacon slab in the smoker, or slices on rack.

- Raise the temperature to 200°F.

- Add moistened wood chips to the smoker receptacle.

- Smoke for 2 hours, monitoring the temperature.

- Remove when the internal temperature reaches 150°F and the smoke has achieved personal preference.

- Cool at room temperature and then refrigerate.

- Slice and fry or cook.

FRESH SAUSAGE

Uncooked and uncured pork is considered fresh and is typically used in sausage making. Fresh sausages include those seasoned and stuffed into casings, or those in bulk form that will be pressed into patties. They are not typically cured or smoked but used right away. Fresh sausages, whether links or patties, should be eaten within 3 days of making them or buying them in a market. They can be frozen for later use but need to be cooked after thawing and not refrozen once thawed. They should be thoroughly cooked before being served. Although some of the following fresh sausages may take a little more time to make than others, they are within your reach of creating for your family. One sample recipe is included for each kind of sausage.

FRESH PORK SAUSAGE PATTIES

1 pound boneless pork shoulder butt

½ teaspoon salt

½ teaspoon ground black pepper

½ teaspoon ground dried thyme

½ teaspoon dried sage

1 teaspoon light brown sugar

¼ teaspoon ground allspice

½ tablespoon minced garlic

1 cup nonchlorinated water

Cut the pork into 1-inch cubes and grind it through the medium plate of a meat grinder. Place in a large bowl. In a separate bowl, combine the salt, pepper, thyme, sage, sugar, allspice, and garlic, and then mix with water. Pour the mixture into the ground pork and mix thoroughly. Shape into 2-ounce patties. Pan fry, turning to brown both sides, for 8 to 10 minutes, or until the internal temperature is at least 160°F. Fresh sausage can be frozen for later use.

Bockwurst: a German-style sausage made from ground veal or veal and pork combined. It is typically flavored with spices and often sold fresh.

HOMEMADE BOCKWURST

1½ pounds boneless pork shoulder butt

3 pounds veal

½ pound pork fat

2 cups whole milk

1½ teaspoons salt

¼ cup minced chives

½ cup minced onion

1 teaspoon white pepper

¾ teaspoon ground cloves

¼ teaspoon ground nutmeg

¼ teaspoon finely chopped chives

4 large eggs, beaten

Cut the pork, veal, and fat into 1-inch cubes and grind twice with the medium plate of a meat grinder. Place in a large bowl. Mix milk, salt, minced chives, onion, pepper, cloves, nutmeg, chopped chives, and eggs together thoroughly. Add spices to meat mixture and mix thoroughly. Grind the mixture through the fine grinder plate. Stuff into casings, making 5-inch lengths. Place the sausage into a pan, cover with water, and bring to a boil. Lower the heat and simmer for 15 minutes. Remove from the heat and serve warm, or let cool in refrigerator and then freeze.

Bratwurst: A German-style sausage made from pork, beef, and veal. It looks like a big hot dog and is flavored with different spices. These can vary between regions and countries. It can be produced as fresh or cooked. It is often made with emulsified meat. You can approximate this by finely grinding the meat and spice mixture in a food processor.

SMOKED BRATWURST

4 pounds boneless pork shoulder butt

1 pound beef chuck

1 pound pork back fat, diced

2 tablespoons noniodized salt

2 tablespoons sugar

2 tablespoons ground white pepper

½ teaspoon cayenne powder

1 tablespoon ground nutmeg

1 teaspoon dried thyme

⅓ teaspoon ground ginger

2 large eggs, beaten

1 cup whole milk

Cut the pork and beef into 1-inch cubes and grind it and the pork back fat through a ¼-inch grinding plate. Regrind through a fine plate and set aside in a large bowl. Thoroughly mix the salt, sugar, pepper, cayenne, nutmeg, thyme, and ginger in nonmetallic container. Mix the eggs thoroughly with milk in a small bowl, then combine with spices and mix thoroughly. Mix the spice mixture into the meat, then place in a food processor in small batches and run until the meat mixture is a pastelike texture. Stuff into pork casings or freeze immediately. The bratwurst must be cooked to an internal temperature of 150°F before serving.

Note: If you desire to smoke the bratwurst, be sure to add 1 level teaspoon of a cure mix to each 5 pounds of meat mixture and mix thoroughly before stuffing and smoking.

Chorizo: Originating in Spain, the term encompasses several types of pork sausage. It can be fresh or cured. Fresh chorizo is similar to Sicilian sausage but is much spicier. Cured or dried chorizo can resemble pepperoni in size and shape, but it has a sharper taste and smell.

BASIC CHORIZO SAUSAGE

5 pounds boneless pork shoulder butt

1 tablespoon chipotle powder

1 tablespoon minced garlic

1 teaspoon dried Mexican oregano

½ teaspoon ground cumin

2 tablespoons chili powder

1 teaspoon ground black pepper

2 tablespoons paprika

3 tablespoons salt

1 cup cider vinegar

Trim the pork and cut into 1-inch cubes. Chill before grinding and then grind it through the ¼-inch meat grinder plate. Reserve the meat in a large bowl. Combine the chipotle powder, garlic, oregano, cumin, chili powder, black pepper, paprika, and salt in nonmetallic container and mix thoroughly. Add the vinegar and spices to the meat and mix thoroughly for at least 2 minutes. Stuff into casings or make into bulk packages. If stuffing, let the chorizo hang in a cooler or refrigerator (if possible) for 8 to 12 hours to dry. It can be kept in the refrigerator for up to 3 days, or in the freezer for 3 months.

Country-style or *breakfast sausage*: One of the most common kinds of sausage found in the United States. It is known by several names, can be made into patties or small links, and is flavored with spices.

COUNTRY SAUSAGE

2½ pounds boneless pork shoulder butt

2½ pounds boneless beef chuck

1 tablespoon salt

2 tablespoons paprika

2 tablespoons crushed garlic

1 tablespoon dried savory

1 tablespoon dried marjoram

1 tablespoon ground black pepper

1 cup nonchlorinated water

Trim fat from the pork and beef and cut into 1-inch cubes. Grind the meat through a medium grinding plate and reserve in a large bowl. Mix the salt, paprika, garlic, savory, marjoram, and pepper in a nonmetallic bowl, then add water and mix thoroughly. Pour the mixture into the pork and beef and mix thoroughly for at least 2 minutes. Stuff into casings. Set the sausage in the refrigerator, covered, for 6 hours before packing for storage. It can be kept up to 3 days in refrigerator or up to 3 months in freezer.

Pork sausage: A fresh, uncooked sausage made entirely from pork and seasonings. It is often sold in bulk, in a chub or links, or as patties.

FRESH PORK SAUSAGE

2 pounds ground pork trimmings
   or boneless pork shoulder butt

2 teaspoons salt

½ teaspoon ground white pepper

1 teaspoon ground black pepper

2 teaspoons dried sage

1 tablespoon brown sugar

¼ teaspoon dried marjoram

⅛ teaspoon cayenne powder

⅛ teaspoon ground cloves

Cut the boneless pork shoulder into 1-inch cubes and grind the meat through a medium plate. Reserve the meat in a large bowl. Mix the salt, white pepper, black pepper, sage, brown sugar, marjoram, cayenne powder, and cloves thoroughly in nonmetallic container. Add the spices to the pork and mix thoroughly. Form the meat into patties and fry in a skillet, turning often, until the internal temperature reaches 160°F. The patties must be cooked before serving.

Kielbasa: It is typically made from coarsely ground lean pork and is sometimes combined with beef and veal, or both. It is similar to Italian sausage in that its name is more of a generic term than a reference to a specific sausage.

POLISH SAUSAGE

5 pounds pork trimmings or boneless
   pork shoulder butt

1 pound lean beef

1 cup water

3 tablespoons salt

¼ cup minced garlic

2 tablespoons ground black pepper

2 tablespoons dried marjoram

Cut pork shoulder and beef into 1-inch cubes and grind the meat through the medium grinding plate. Reserve the meat in a large bowl. Mix the water, salt, garlic, black pepper, and marjoram together in a small bowl and add to meat mixture. Regrind the mixture through a ¼-inch plate and stuff into casings. Refrigerate immediately. It can be kept for up to 3 days in the refrigerator or up to 3 months in the freezer. It must be cooked before serving.

Italian-style sausage: A traditional pure pork sausage with spices added for flavoring. It is a fresh sausage that must be fully cooked before eating and can have either a hot or sweet taste.

SWEET ITALIAN SAUSAGE

5 pounds pork trimmings or boneless pork shoulder butt

1 pound pork back fat

3½ tablespoons salt

5 teaspoons cracked fennel seed

2 tablespoons paprika

3 teaspoons ground black pepper

2 tablespoons sugar

2 teaspoons minced garlic

1 teaspoon dried oregano

1 teaspoon dried sweet basil

1 cup nonchlorinated water

Cut pork and fat into 1-inch cubes and grind meat and fat through the ¼-inch plate of meat grinder. Reserve the meat in a large bowl. Combine the salt, fennel, paprika, pepper, sugar, garlic, oregano, and basil in a nonmetallic container and mix thoroughly with water. Add the mixture to the meat, mix, and regrind through a ¼-inch diameter plate. Stuff into casings or make bulk packages. No smoking is necessary as this is a fresh sausage. Cook before serving. It can be kept in the refrigerator for up to 3 days or in the freezer for 3 months.

SPICY ITALIAN SAUSAGE

5 pounds pork trimmings
  or boneless pork shoulder butt

½ pound pork back fat, diced

½ teaspoon cayenne pepper

2 tablespoons hot red pepper flakes

3 tablespoons paprika

2 tablespoons fennel seeds, crushed

2 teaspoons dried thyme

2 teaspoons minced garlic

4 tablespoons fresh basil leaves

4 tablespoons fresh oregano leaves

3 tablespoons salt

2 tablespoons sugar

2 teaspoons ground black pepper

½ teaspoon ground nutmeg

¼ cup red wine vinegar

1 cup water

Cube the pork shoulder into 1-inch pieces and grind it and the back fat through a coarse plate into a large bowl. Add the cayenne pepper, red pepper flakes, paprika, fennel seeds, thyme, garlic, basil, oregano, salt, sugar, pepper, and nutmeg, and mix thoroughly. Grind again through a medium plate. Add the vinegar and water and mix thoroughly. Stuff the mixture into casings and twist into 6-inch links. Refrigerate or freeze until ready to cook. Cook at an internal temperature of 150°F. If you smoke it, smoke at 140°F for proper color development and then raise the temperature to 170°F, until the internal temperature reaches 155°F.

Liverwurst: A popular German-style sausage made from finely ground pork and pork liver. It can be stuffed into a nonedible casing but must be thoroughly cooked before being served. Spices are used to give distinct flavors. The term is sometimes interchanged with Braunschweiger because of the similarities between the two in production, texture, and taste.

LIVERWURST

3 pounds pork shoulder butt

2 pounds pork liver

1 medium onion, grated

2 tablespoons salt

1 teaspoon dried marjoram

1 teaspoon allspice

1 tablespoon ground black pepper

½ teaspoon dried ground sage

1 cup water

Cut the pork and liver into 1-inch cubes. Place the liver in a skillet over medium heat and simmer for 3 minutes, then remove from the heat and let cool. Grind the pork and liver twice with a fine grinder plate or pulse in a food processor until finely ground. Mix the onion, salt, marjoram, allspice, pepper, and sage with water in a small bowl, then add that mixture to the ground meat and mix thoroughly. Stuff in casings, and then simmer the sausages in water until the internal temperature reaches a minimum of 152°F. When finished, remove from water and let cool to room temperature. Package and refrigerate. Serve cold or freeze.

BRAUNSCHWEIGER

10 pounds pork trimmings
and boneless pork shoulder butt

10 pounds pork liver

1 pound fat bacon

⅔ cup salt

4 tablespoons ground white pepper

3 ounces soy protein (optional)

1 medium onion, grated

1 teaspoon ground nutmeg

1½ teaspoons ground ginger

1 tablespoon cure (6 percent)

Cut the pork and liver into 1-inch cubes. Grind pork trimmings, liver, and bacon to a very fine consistency. In a large bowl, mix the meat with salt, pepper, soy protein, onion, nutmeg, ginger, and cure. Stuff in moisture-proof fibrous casing and cook in a 165°F water bath for 1½ hours or until the internal temperature of sausage reaches 155°F. Remove from heat and chill rapidly in water.

Thuringer sausage: A lightly smoked, German-style sausage mostly made from pork and similar to summer sausage. It is often semidry and is more perishable than other cured sausages, even though, technically, it is cured. Some are not fermented and are sold fresh.

THURINGER SAUSAGE

2 teaspoons black peppercorns

4 pounds boneless pork shoulder

1 pound pork back fat

3 tablespoons Fermento

3 tablespoons salt

2 teaspoons cure

2 tablespoons sugar

½ teaspoon dry ground mustard

2 teaspoons ground coriander

2 teaspoons allspice

In a small bowl, cover the peppercorns with warm water and soak for a minimum of 1 hour. Cube the pork shoulder and fat into 1-inch pieces, and then grind through a medium grinding plate. Dissolve the Fermento in ½ cup water, stirring to a thin paste. In another small bowl, mix the salt, cure, sugar, drained peppercorns, mustard, coriander, and allspice thoroughly. Add spice mix and Fermento to meat and mix together. Refrigerate for 3 days or ferment at 85ºF for a minimum of 24 hours. Regrind the meat through a fine plate. Stuff the mixture into sausage casings, tie the ends, and hang on smoke sticks. Let them dry for minimum of 10 hours at 65 to 70ºF. Then cold smoke below 100º F for 5 hours (see page 169). Raise the smoker temperature to 180ºF and bring the internal sausage temperature to 150ºF. Place in a cold-water bath to cool completely, then refrigerate.

COOKED AND SMOKED SAUSAGES

Cooked sausages are usually made from fresh meats that are cured during processing, fully cooked, and/or smoked. All cooked sausages should be refrigerated until eaten. Because they are fully cooked, they are ready to eat once opened, although you may prefer to serve them warm or hot.

Frankfurters (sometimes called the common hot dog), bologna, and other sausages are cured and cooked sausages made using a cure. They are typically created by emulsifying the meat prior to stuffing into casings. Emulsifying meat is a process that grinds the meat multiple times or purees it. This helps to evenly distribute the fat to make a smooth, creamy paste that creates a very fine meat texture and uniform color. Emulsifying meat will take several more steps than simply grinding meat for fresh sausages but can be done in your home. Temperature is an important part of this and, generally, the colder the meat the better result you will have. You can follow the steps here to emulsify the meat for hot dogs, bratwursts, or bologna-style sausages.

BASIC EMULSION STEPS

- Cut the meat and fat into cubes and grind them through the grinder's large die.

- Season the meat and fat with salt, cure, and spices, and mix thoroughly.

- Cool the meat in the refrigerator, covered, for 4 hours.

- Remove the meat and regrind, adding nonchlorinated crushed ice to keep the consistency moist (you can add up to 1½ cups ice or water without affecting the result).

- Regrind through the small die. (It may be easier to grind if chilled between grindings.)

- Place the meat mixture in a food processor and grind until a stiff, batterlike consistency.

- Add dry milk powder to stabilize the emulsion and aid moisture retention.

- Refrigerate the mixture until ready for stuffing into casings.

Some examples of cooked sausages (using emulsifying steps) include

- *Frankfurters*: Also known as the common hot dog, they are processed and contain mostly water and fat and have a soft, even texture and flavor. Homemade frankfurters can be made with a blend of pork, beef, and/or poultry meat.

- *Bologna*: A generic term for a fully cooked, mildly seasoned sausage made from low-value pieces of pork, beef, or both. It can be eaten cold or reheated. It is typically produced in large-diameter rings or chubs, which give it several distinctive styles and shape, although they are much the same as hot dogs.

- *New England sausage*: Also known as *Berliner*, this sausage is made from coarse-ground pork with pieces of ham or chopped beef interspersed within it. Generally, it is stuffed into large casings.

• *Mettwurst*: A strongly flavored German-style sausage made from raw minced pork and preserved by smoking and curing. Although it is smoked, it needs to be cooked thoroughly before serving. It can have either a soft or hard texture, depending on the length of smoking time used. This is a smoked sausage, and if you make it, you *must* use a cure product and follow good smoking procedures.

METTWURST SAUSAGE

3 pounds pork shoulder butt	½ teaspoon dried marjoram
1 pound veal	½ teaspoon ground caraway seeds
1 pound beef chuck	1 teaspoon whole mustard seeds
2 tablespoons salt	1 teaspoon ground celery seeds
1 tablespoon ground white pepper	1 teaspoon commercial cure (if smoked)
1 teaspoon ground coriander	
1 teaspoon allspice	

Cut the pork, veal, and chuck into 1-inch cubes and grind through a medium plate. Reserve the meat in a large bowl. In a small bowl, mix the salt, white pepper, coriander, allspice, marjoram, caraway seeds, mustard seeds, celery seeds, and cure until combined. Add the spices to the meat mixture and mix thoroughly. When mixed, regrind the full mixture through a fine plate and stuff in casings. Smoke the sausage at 100 to 120ºF for a minimum of 6 hours, then increase the smoker temperature to 160ºF and continue smoking until reaching an internal temperature of 150ºF. Rinse the sausages with cool water to allow flavors to develop. Place in a cooler or refrigerator for 12 hours before packing or freezing.

HOT DOG RECIPE

3 pounds pork shoulder butt	2 teaspoons ground coriander
2 pounds beef chuck	1 tablespoon onion powder
3 tablespoons paprika	1 tablespoon ground mace
3 tablespoons corn syrup	1 tablespoon ground white pepper
2 teaspoons garlic powder	1 teaspoon cure
1 tablespoon ground dried mustard	1 cup nonfat dried milk powder
1 tablespoon salt	2 egg whites
2 teaspoons finely ground black pepper	1½ cups ice water

Cut the pork and beef into 1-inch cubes. Grind twice through the smallest grinder plate. Refrigerate in a large bowl for 2 hours between grindings. In a medium bowl, mix the paprika, corn syrup, garlic powder, mustard, salt, black pepper, coriander, onion powder, mace, white pepper, cure, and dried milk powder thoroughly, and then incorporate the egg whites. Mix the spices with meat and refrigerate for 30 minutes. Grind the mixture again through a fine grinding plate. Chill. Emulsify small batches in a food processor, adding ice water as needed until a pastelike consistency. Repeat with the remaining mixture until it's all emulsified, and keep the mixture cool until ready to stuff into casings. After stuffing, they are ready for meat smoker. Or cook them for eating by simmering in water until they reach internal temperature of 152ºF.

DRY AND SEMIDRY SAUSAGES

Dry and semidry pork sausages can be made from fresh pork that is ground, seasoned, and cured during processing. This mixture can be stuffed into either natural or synthetic casings, fermented, often smoked, and air-dried. True dry sausages are generally not cooked and may require long drying periods of between 21 and 90 days, depending on their diameter.

The distinctive flavor of these sausages is due to the lactic acid produced by fermentation. This occurs after the meat is stuffed into casings and the bacteria metabolize the sugars, producing acids and other compounds as byproducts and the resulting tangy flavor.

Semidry sausages are often fermented and cooked in a smokehouse. Both dry and semidry sausages are ready to eat and do not require heating before serving, although a cool temperature or refrigeration is recommended for storage. Below is a list of semidry sausages:

- *Pepperoni*: A hotly spiced Italian-style sausage made from coarsely ground, fermented pork with seasonings added. It is a lean, dry sausage with a fat content less than 30 percent, and it increases in flavor as it ages in the drying process. It can be made with pork, beef, or a combination of 70 percent pork and 30 percent beef.

- *Salami*: A generic term used for products that have similar characteristics. It is made from pork, beef, or both. They can be found in many sizes and shapes, and they may be dry and quite hard.

TRADITIONAL SALAMI

4 pounds boneless pork shoulder

1 pound pork back fat

¼ cup salt

1 teaspoon cure

¼ cup Bactoferm F-RM-52,
  starter culture

¼ cup nonchlorinated water

½ cup nonfat dry milk powder

3 tablespoons sugar

1½ tablespoons ground fennel

4 teaspoons ground black pepper

1 teaspoon minced garlic

Cut the pork and fat into 1-inch cubes but keep them separate (this will keep the fat distinct from the meat in the finished product). Combine the pork shoulder with salt and cure thoroughly and grind with small die. Reserve in a large bowl. Mix in the back fat and cure and cool in the refrigerator until ready for mixing. Dissolve the Bactoferm in water and add to the meat. Then mix in the dry milk powder, sugar, fennel, black pepper, and garlic. Stuff the sausage into casings and twist into 8-inch links. Use a sterile pin or needle to poke holes in casings to remove air pockets and help drying. Weigh each link and record the results. Cover the sausage links with clean towel and allow to sit at room temperature (80 to 85ºF) for 12 hours for bacteria to grow and produce lactic acid. Then hang the sausages in drying area at 60ºF with 60 to 70 percent humidity that is free of insects, pests, and rodents. Dry until they're completely firm or have lost 30 percent of their weight (about 6 to 14 weeks). Store sausages at temperatures of 50 to 60ºF and with less than 75 percent humidity.

PEPPERONI SAUSAGE

4 pounds pork shoulder

1 pound beef chuck

4 tablespoons salt

2 tablespoons cure

¼ cup Bactoferm F-RM-52 starter culture

¼ cup nonchlorinated water

4 tablespoons sugar

1 tablespoon ground black pepper

2 tablespoons paprika

¾ cup nonfat dry milk powder

1½ teaspoons ground fennel

2 teaspoons cayenne pepper

Cut the pork and beef into 1-inch cubes, place in a large bowl, and mix with salt and cure. Grind through the smallest die. In a small bowl, dissolve the Bactoferm in water. Mix the sugar, black pepper, paprika, dry milk powder, fennel, and cayenne pepper thoroughly. Mix spices with Bactoferm thoroughly and mix into the meat. Stuff the mixture into sausage casings and twist into 10-inch lengths. Using a sterile pin or needle, poke holes all over the casings to remove any air pockets and help with drying. Weigh each link and record the results. Hang the links at room temperature (80 to 85°F) for 12 hours to allow bacteria to produce lactic acid. Then hang the sausages in a drying area at 60°F with 60 to 70 percent humidity that is free of insects, pests, and rodents. Dry until they're completely firm or have lost 30 percent of their weight (about 6 to 14 weeks). Store the sausages at temperatures of 50 to 60°F with less than 75 percent humidity.

Landjäger: A traditional Swiss-German dried sausage that is similar in taste to dried salami. It is made from equal portions of pork and beef, with lard or fat and sugar and spices added. The meat is pressed into small casings for making links, usually 6- to 8-inch lengths. They are then pressed into a mold before drying, which gives them their characteristic rectangular shape. After drying, they can keep without refrigeration if needed.

LANDJÄGER SAUSAGE

3 pounds pork shoulder

1 pound beef chuck

¼ cup salt

1 teaspoon cure

3 tablespoons sugar

4 teaspoons ground black pepper

¼ teaspoon ground caraway seed

¼ teaspoon cardamom

¼ cup Fermento

1 teaspoon ground nutmeg

⅓ cup nonchlorinated water

2 tablespoons corn syrup

Cut the pork and beef into 1-inch cubes and grind through fine grinding plate. Reserve the meat in a large bowl. In a small bowl, mix the salt, cure, sugar, black pepper, caraway seed, cardamom, Fermento, and nutmeg together thoroughly. Mix the water and corn syrup together in another small bowl, then mix with the spices thoroughly. Add to the meat mixture and incorporate thoroughly. Cool in the refrigerator for 30 minutes. Stuff the casings, but not tightly, and make 8-inch links. Use a sterile pin or needle to prick any air pockets. Place the stuffed sausage between two clean weights to flatten them. Allow to sit and ferment for 72 hours at room temperature (68 to 70ºF with 90 to 95 percent humidity). Remove the weights and clean off any accumulated slime on the links. Weigh each link and record the results. Dry at room temperature until casings are dry to the touch or place in smoker with vent open at 140ºF, without smoke, until the casings are dry to the touch. Tie a cooking string or cord around each link and hang from smoke racks. Cold smoke at 68ºF for 4 hours to prevent mold growth. After the casings feel dry, start to smoke at 145ºF for 2 hours with the vent full open. Raise the temperature to 170ºF with or without smoke (your preference) and continue until reaching an internal temperature of 160ºF. Remove and allow to cool. Then hang the sausages in a drying area free of insects, pests, and rodents at 60ºF with 60 to 70 percent humidity for 14 to 15 days, until hard. Dry until they're completely firm or have lost 30 percent of their weight (about 6 weeks). Store sausages at temperatures of 50 to 60ºF and with less than 75 percent humidity.

OTHER SAUSAGES

With more than 200 types of sausages commonly available, you can produce a wide variety in your home. While you may start with making only one or two types of sausage, in time you may venture to others. Those with pork used as the main ingredient include the following:

- *Alessandri*: An Italian-style member of the salami family made with highly seasoned cured pork.

- *Arles*: A French-style salami that contains coarsely chopped pork and beef.

- *Blood and tongue sausage*: Contains cooked pork tongues and hog blood.

- *Bloodwurst* or *blood sausage*: Sausage made of pig blood, pork meat, ham fat, gelatin-based cuts.

POTATO SAUSAGE

3 pounds meat (pork head)

½ cup nonchlorinated water

10 pounds potatoes,
  peeled and grated

2 onions, ground

Pepper, salt, dried sweet marjoram
  to taste

In a large pot, cook the meat in water until done. Reserve the accumulated cooking liquid. Allow the meat to cool, then grind. Mix the ground meat in a large bowl with potatoes, onions, and spices. Add broth until mixture looks like cooked oatmeal. Stuff in casings, then heat in hot water.

BLOOD SAUSAGE

1 pint pig blood

1 pint milk or water

½ teaspoon ground black pepper

¼ teaspoon ground nutmeg

1½ teaspoons ground cloves

1½ teaspoons ground allspice

1 tablespoon salt

1 cup quick-cooking rolled oats

5 cups flour, plus up to 1 cup more
  as needed

Mix all the ingredients together. If the batter is too runny, add additional flour, up to 1 more cup. Drop by large spoonfuls into a large kettle of salted boiling water. Cook until brown throughout. Remove from the water and eat hot with butter and syrup.

Ham and cheese loaf: Contains pieces of finely ground ham with cheese.

HAM LOAF

¼ pound cooked lean ham

1 cup bread crumbs

3 large eggs

2 tablespoons chili sauce

1 cup ground carrots

½ teaspoon salt

½ teaspoon ground black pepper

2 cups milk

¼ cup grated cheese

Orange slices (optional), for serving

Pear halves (optional), for serving

Mint jelly (optional), for serving

Sweet cherries (optional), for serving

Preheat the oven to 375°F. Chop ham finely and place in a large bowl. In a large bowl, mix bread crumbs, eggs, chili sauce, carrots, salt, pepper, and milk thoroughly. Mix in the ham and cheese. Place in 9×5-inch loaf pan or mold and bake for 20 to 30 minutes. Serve with a garnish of orange slices, or with pear halves filled with mint jelly and topped with sweet cherries.

Loaf Variations

- *Honey loaf*: A mixture of pork, beef, honey, and spices.

- *Linguisa*: A Portuguese pork sausage cured in brine with seasonings added.

- *Liver loaf*: A sandwich-shaped liver sausage that is similar in flavor to liverwurst.

- *Mortadella*: A dry sausage containing pork, beef, and cubes of pork fat.

- *Salsiccia*: A fresh Italian sausage made of finely ground pork.

- *Smoky links*: Smoked, cooked links made from pork and beef, with spices added.

- *Weisswurst*: A fresh German-style sausage that is mildly spicy and made of pork and veal.

Chapter 8

COOKING WITH PORK

You have reached the end of your work, and now is the time to reap your reward with hearty and tasteful meals. The range of uses with pork is almost limitless and maybe only by your imagination. You have butchered your own animal, you have cut apart the carcass, you have preserved much of the meat for later use, and now you can begin to experiment with cooking.

This chapter will focus on different styles of cooking in relation to using pork. Because the number of recipes is almost endless, we will explore some of the more common ones but provide a framework for alterations as you proceed.

PORK COOKING TIME AND TEMPERATURE CHART

Roasting

	Weight in Pounds	Oven Temperature	Interior Temperature When Done	Time per Pound in Minutes
Fresh				
Loin—Center	3–4	350°F	185°F	35–40
Whole	8–15	350	185	15–20
Ends	3–4	350	185	50–55
Shoulder—Whole	12–14	350	185	30–35
Boned and rolled	4–6	350	185	40–45
Cushion	4–6	350	185	35–40
Spareribs	1½–1¾	350	185	40–45
Pork butt	4–6	350	185	45–50
Ham	10–18	350	185	30–35
Smoked				
Ham—Whole	10–12	350	170	25
Half	6	350	170	30
Shank end	3	350	170	40
Butt end	3	350	170	45
Picnic	3–10	350	170	35

Broiling

	Weight in Pounds	Total Cooking Time
Ham slice—½ inch	¾–1	20
1 inch	1½–2	25–30

Braising

	Average Weight or Thickness	Cooking Time in Minutes
Chops	¾–1½ inches	45–60
Spareribs	2–3 pounds	90
Tenderloin—Whole	¾–1 pound	45–60
Fillets	½ inch	30
Shoulder steak	¾ inch	30–45

PIG'S BRAIN

At the time of this writing, there is no scientific evidence available that eating the brains from pigs is detrimental to your health or can produce a food-borne illness. In fact, they can be found in specialty markets and can be used as a stir-fry staple. Perhaps not such a favorite in the United States, but that is mainly due to familiarity and acceptance. Although pig brains can be safely eaten, they do need to be prepared carefully.

To precook the brains, first wash them thoroughly in cold water and then allow them to soak in a large bowl, covered with cold water, for 1 to 2 hours. Place in a pot. Add 2 quarts of water, 2 teaspoons salt, 2 tablespoons lemon juice or vinegar, and any desired seasonings. (The acid helps to keep the brains white and firm.) Simmer for 20 minutes and drain.

BREADED BRAINS

1 pound pork brains, cooked and drained

1 egg

1 tablespoon whole milk

½ teaspoon salt

½ teaspoon ground black pepper

½ cup dry bread crumbs, crushed

1 cup lard

Remove the outer membrane of the brain. Slice into ½-inch-thick strips. Beat the egg in a small bowl and then mix in the milk, salt, and pepper. Pour the mixture into a shallow dish. Pour the bread crumbs into another shallow dish. In a skillet over medium heat, heat the lard until melted and hot. Dip the strips into liquid mixture and then coat with bread crumbs. Fry in the skillet until brown. Remove and season to taste. They can be eaten with scrambled eggs and/or vegetables.

BRAIN RISSOLES

2 tablespoons butter or margarine

2 tablespoons all-purpose white flour

¼ teaspoon salt

⅛ teaspoon ground black pepper

1 cup whole milk

1 pound pork brains,
  cooked and drained

¾ teaspoon salt

2 tablespoons chopped green pepper

For pastry dough:

2 cups sifted white flour

¾ teaspoon salt

⅔ cup shortening

5 tablespoons nonchlorinated water

In a medium saucepan, melt the butter over low heat. Stir in the flour, salt, and pepper. Cook over medium heat, stirring constantly, until the mixture is smooth and bubbly. Remove from the heat. Gradually stir in the milk, return to heat, and bring to a boil, stirring constantly. Boil 1 minute then remove the sauce from the heat and let cool.

Remove the outer membrane of the brain. Slice into pieces and grind in food processor.

Add salt, green pepper, and the sauce to the food processor and pulse to combine. Form into small balls.

For the pastry dough, mix the flour and salt together and blend in shortening using a pastry cutter, a fork, or your clean fingers. Add water until the mixture holds together. Roll out half of the pastry dough ⅛ inch thick. Place the balls of meat on the pastry equal distances apart. Roll out the remaining pastry and drape it over the meat balls, lined up with the bottom pastry. Cut out around each meatball with a round cutter. Press the upper and lower edges together. Bake until at 450ºF for 15 minutes, or deep-fry at 375ºF for 10 minutes.

PIG'S HEART

The heart can be used but is generally less tender than the liver. It has an excellent flavor when cooked with moist heat, chopped, and added with other ingredients to casseroles, or ground up to use in sausage making. Another variation of a pig heart is to slice it open, fill it with dressing, stitch it shut with cooking thread, and then roast it with moist heat.

HEART GOULASH

1 tablespoon lard

1 cup cooked, chopped pig heart

1 cup cooked, chopped pork shoulder

½ onion, chopped

1 cup water

1¼ teaspoons salt

½ cup diced carrot

1 cup diced celery

½ cup diced tomato

½ cup sour cream

2 tablespoons cold water

2 tablespoons flour

2½ cups cooked rice or noodles

In a skillet over medium heat, melt the lard. Brown the heart, pork, and onion in the lard, then add water, salt, carrots, and celery. Cook for 20 minutes or until the vegetables are tender. Add the tomatoes and sour cream. In a small bowl, mix the water and flour to a smooth paste and then blend into the meat mixture. Cook over low heat until thickened. Serve with cooked rice or noodles.

STUFFED HEART

1 pig heart

8 ounces bread stuffing

2 tablespoons lard

2 tablespoons flour

1½ cups water

Slice open the heart halfway. Wash it thoroughly and then fill with stuffing. Tie it together firmly with cooking string. In a metal skillet, melt the lard and heat until shimmering. Roll the heart in flour, and then brown in the hot lard. Season with salt and pepper. Add the water, cover tightly, and simmer on low heat for 3 hours or until tender. Thicken the liquid as needed with additional flour.

TONGUE

Tongue can be used fresh, pickled, corned, or smoked. Smoked or pickled tongue may require soaking several hours before cooking. Tongue should be cooked slowly in liquid until tender. Then remove the skin and cut away the roots that attach it to the jaw.

For fresh tongue, first cover it with water in a cooking pan and add 1 teaspoon salt for each quart of water added. Then cover tightly and simmer until tender. Allow 1 to 2 hours for a pork tongue.

If the tongue has been pickled, place it in a cooking pan and cover with cold water. Then heat to boiling. Pour off the water and cover with fresh water. Cover tightly and simmer 3 to 4 hours or until tender.

Smoked tongue should be placed in a cooking pan and covered with cold water. Then heat to boiling. Reduce heat and cover tightly. Then simmer 4 hours or until tender.

BAKED TONGUE AND NOODLES

¾ pound cooked pork tongue, sliced

3½ cups cooked noodles

2 cups cooked tomatoes

¼ cup cracker crumbs

1 tablespoon butter

Preheat the oven to 350ºF. Arrange layers of tongue and noodles in a baking dish. Add the tomatoes and cover with crumbs. Dot with butter. Bake for 30 minutes.

PIG TONGUE

1 fresh pork tongue

2 medium onions, sliced

1 carrot

¾ cup diced celery and leaves

1 tablespoon ground parsley

8 whole peppercorns

1 teaspoon salt

Place the ingredients in dutch oven or similar pan, using just enough water to cover tongue. Simmer for 3 to 4 hours or until tongue is tender. Drain off the water and serve the tongue sliced, hot or cold.

PIG'S KIDNEY

The kidneys are high in protein content and highly nutritious. They can be broiled, skewered, or sliced or chopped to be included in casseroles or stews. They should be sliced open and thoroughly washed on the insides before using.

STEWED KIDNEYS

2 pork kidneys

1 teaspoon salt

1 teaspoon ground black pepper

1½ tablespoons liquid lard

1 tablespoon chopped fresh parsley

½ teaspoon dried thyme

1 bay leaf, crumbled

1 cup water

1 teaspoon vinegar

Remove the outer skin from the kidneys. Slice each kidney in half, wash thoroughly, and remove the white tubes. Slice into ¼-inch pieces and season with salt and pepper. Let stand for 30 minutes, and then drain and dry with a paper towel. Heat the lard in a skillet over medium heat, then add the kidneys and cook with herbs until tender. Add water and vinegar and heat thoroughly. Serve immediately.

PORK AND KIDNEY PIE

1½ pounds pork shoulder

½ pound pork kidneys

2 cups flour

1 teaspoon salt

1 teaspoon ground black pepper

1 tablespoon chopped onion

1 tablespoon minced parsley

½ pound mushrooms, sliced

For the pastry dough:

2 cups sifted white flour

¾ teaspoon salt

⅔ cup shortening

5 tablespoons nonchlorinated water

Preheat the oven to 350ºF. Cut the pork and kidney into ½-inch cubes. Mix the flour with salt and pepper in a shallow dish and then roll the pork pieces in the mix to coat evenly. In a greased casserole dish, arrange the meat in an even layer and add onion, parsley, mushrooms, and enough water to cover the meat completely. Cover tightly with a lid or foil and cook for 1 hour, or until meat is tender.

For the pastry dough, mix the flour and salt together in a large bowl and blend in the shortening using a pastry cutter, a fork, or your fingers. Add water until the mixture holds together.

Roll out the pastry dough large enough to cover the casserole dish. Remove the casserole dish from the oven. Remove the cover and carefully replace it with pastry, pricking the crust to allow steam to escape. Return to oven, increase the heat to 450ºF, and bake for 15 minutes or until the crust is browned.

PIG'S LIVER

The liver metabolizes sugars into glucose that provides energy to the pig's body systems. It should have a bright, healthy look and be completely free of abscesses in order to use it.

The liver is a versatile byproduct that can be sliced and fried fresh or frozen for later use. It can also be ground up and used in sausage making, pan loaves, or spreads.

SAVORY LIVER

1½ pounds pork liver, sliced into ¼-inch strips

¼ cup chopped onion

2 teaspoons chopped fresh parsley

2 tablespoons butter

2 tablespoons flour

1 teaspoon salt

1 teaspoon ground black pepper

3 tablespoons vinegar

2½ cups vegetable broth

In a deep skillet over medium heat, brown the onion and parsley in butter. Stir in the flour, salt, pepper, and vinegar, and then add the broth gradually, stirring constantly. Cook until thickened. Add the liver to the gravy and cook, covered, for 15 minutes, turning once.

LIVER CASSEROLE

1 pound pork liver

¾ cup tomato sauce

1 teaspoon salt

1 teaspoon ground black pepper

1 teaspoon Worcestershire sauce

Preheat the oven 350ºF. Wash the liver thoroughly. Cut into 1½-inch cubes and place in a greased casserole dish. Add the tomato sauce, salt, and pepper; cover with a lid or foil and bake for 30 minutes. Add the Worcestershire sauce just before serving.

BRAISED LIVER

2 pounds pork liver

4 slices bacon

1 onion, sliced

2 teaspoons Worcestershire sauce

2 tablespoons ketchup

1 tablespoon chopped green pepper

1 teaspoon salt

1 teaspoon ground black pepper

½ cup water

Preheat the oven to 300°F. Place the liver in a greased baking dish and cover with bacon slices. Mix the onion, Worcestershire sauce, ketchup, green pepper, salt, and black pepper together in a small bowl and then pour over the liver. Add water to the pan, cover tightly, and bake for 1½ hours. Remove the cover for the last 15 minutes of baking to brown the bacon.

LUNGS

You can eat pig lungs solely as a dish by themselves or ground up for inclusion in sausage making.

Whichever option you choose, the lungs must be washed and cleaned thoroughly inside and out. The easiest way to do this is to slice each lung open into halves, making four pieces. Use clean water to rinse and rub the inside cavities. Dry off with clean towels and place on a hard cutting surface. Use a food mallet to beat the pieces and remove most of the air that may be trapped inside. Trim out the main bronchi and any cartilaginous parts. You should be left with four even-sized pieces. You can then slice them and use like a pork roast since it is roughly about the same consistency and firmness. You can also cut it into cubes to mix with sausage.

PIG STOMACH

Your pig's stomach is likely to have feed material in it, such as grains and grass, since it was likely eating until shortly before you butchered it. This means you will need to thoroughly clean out the stomach contents before using it.

- Begin by rinsing the stomach inside and outside to remove any particles attached to it.

- Next, vigorously rub table salt over the entire exterior surface.

- To keep stomach intact, make a cut about 4 inches long in one end of the stomach and turn the stomach inside out, or slice the stomach into two halves.

- Rinse thoroughly with cold water and then let drain.

- Sprinkle the entire interior surface with salt and rub in vigorously.

- Let sit for 15 minutes.

- Rinse well under running water or in a bowl of clean water and then let drain.

- Use a table knife to scrape the stomach's interior side to remove any fats and other impurities on the lining.

- Rinse with cold water.

- Repeat the above steps until any stomach odor is gone. It may take two to three repeats.

- When the smell is gone, leave the stomach intact or slice it in half, making two pieces.

- Bring a pot of water to boiling and add the stomach pieces. Boil for 5 minutes to cook away any slimy impurities. (The stomach should be a pale, milky color when finished.)

- Drain the stomach pieces and let cool. Dry with a clean paper towel.

- Package and freeze or use within 2 days if not frozen.

PIG STOMACH SOUP

1 cleaned, cooked pig stomach

4 cups nonchlorinated water

3 tablespoons salt

3 tablespoons corn flour

4 teaspoons whole peppercorns, crushed

1 teaspoon ground white pepper

1 tablespoon chopped coriander

Cut the cooked stomach into strips ¼-inch wide, 2 inches long. Add water to the soup pot and mix in salt, corn flour, peppercorns, white pepper, and coriander. Add the stomach strips and simmer, covered, for 1½ hours. Serve hot.

STUFFED PIG STOMACH

2 pounds pork sausage

2 stalks celery, diced

2 eggs

2 potatoes, diced

1 medium onion, chopped

1 teaspoon salt

1 teaspoon ground black pepper

1 whole pig stomach, cleaned

Preheat the oven to 350°F. Combine pork sausage and celery, eggs, potatoes, onion, salt, and pepper thoroughly in nonmetallic container. Place the stomach on clean cutting board and stitch one end closed with cooking thread. Stuff the ingredients into the stomach and then stitch the opening closed. Place in casserole dish, cover, and bake for 2½ hours. Uncover for the last 20 to 30 minutes to brown the outer skin. Slice and serve.

PIG'S HEAD

After removing the head, follow these steps:

- Rinse the head well with cold water and pat dry.

- Place the head in a colander in the sink and pour boiling water over the inside of neck to remove any particles.

- Slice the underside of head and rub half of the recipe mixture below into the opening.

- Rub the remaining mixture onto the skin. Place the head upright on a rack in a large baking pan.

- Bake at 375°F for 1½ hours.

- Lower the heat to 320°F and cook for 2 more hours, or until cooked through.

- Baste the skin well every 30 minutes with the honey-water mixture.

- When finished baking, remove to a platter and garnish.

- Slice the meat into pieces and serve with sweet vegetables and a sweet sauce.

PIG'S HEAD

¼ teaspoon ground cinnamon

¼ teaspoon ground cloves

¼ teaspoon fennel seed, toasted and ground

¼ teaspoon ground star anise

¼ teaspoon peppercorns, toasted and ground

2 tablespoons salt

½ cup brown bean sauce

1 pig's head, cleaned

1 cup honey

1 cup nonchlorinated water

Combine cinnamon, cloves, fennel seed, star anise, peppercorns, salt, and bean sauce thoroughly. Use this spice mixture as outlined above. Mix honey and water together in a medium bowl to use for basting. Use as directed above.

SCRAPPLE

1 pig's head, scraped and cleaned

4¼ quarts nonchlorinated water

4 teaspoons salt

4 teaspoons ground black pepper

1 teaspoon powdered dried sage

3 cups yellow cornmeal

Separate the head into halves. Remove the eyes and brains. Place in a large kettle and cover with cold water. Simmer gently for 2 to 3 hours, or until the meat falls from the bones. Carefully skim the grease from the surface, then remove the bones and discard. Remove the meat, chop fine, and return to the liquid. Season with salt, pepper, and sage. Sift in the cornmeal, stirring constantly, and cook until the mixture is thickened to the consistency of soft mush. Cook slowly for 1 hour over low heat. When sufficiently cooked, pour into greased oblong pans and store in the refrigerator until ready to use. To serve, heat a skillet over medium heat. Cut the scrapple into thin slices and fry until crisp and brown.

PIG SPLEEN

Before cooking the spleen:

- Wash it thorough in cold water and pat dry.

- Lay it on a clean cutting board and trim off the outer membrane.

PIG SPLEEN ROLLO

1 pig spleen, cleaned

1 teaspoon salt

1 teaspoon ground black pepper

2 slices bacon, fresh or smoked

4 large fresh sage leaves

4 chicken bouillon cubes

1 quart nonchlorinated water

1 green pepper

1 medium red onion

Preheat the oven to 350°F. Lay spleen on a clean cutting board and slice in half lengthwise. Sprinkle salt and pepper evenly over surfaces. Lay the bacon strips on the spleen and top with sage leaves. Roll the spleen tightly and skewer with wood or metal picks. Dissolve the bouillon cubes in water and pour into oven-safe casserole dish. Slice the green pepper into strips and place the spleen slices and pepper strips into the dish. Cover and bake for 1½ hours. Serve with raw onion slices.

PIG SPLEEN PÂTÉ

1 pig spleen, cleaned

1 small onion, minced

1 tablespoon butter

1 ounce Cognac

1 cup white wine

1 anchovy filet, minced

Chop the spleen finely or grind in food processor. Mince the onion and sauté in butter in skillet over medium heat. When it browns, add the spleen and sprinkle with Cognac. After the Cognac evaporates, add the white wine and continue simmering until the spleen is about half done. Add the minced anchovy filet. Stir constantly, moistening with wine as necessary, until done, about 10 minutes. Allow to cool and then serve on toast or thinly sliced bread.

BONES AND MARROW

The bones are useful for the marrow they contain, which can be used for soup, stocks, or additional flavor in other dishes.

ROASTED PIG BONES

3 to 4 pounds pork bones

4 large portabello mushrooms, stems removed

2 teaspoons sea salt

1½ tablespoons extra virgin olive oil

2 teaspoons fresh lemon juice

1 cup chopped fresh parsley

2 teaspoons capers

4- to 6½-inch-thick slices of crusty bread, toasted

Preheat the oven to 450°F. On a foil-lined baking sheet or in a large metal oven-safe skillet, arrange the bones cut-side up. Add mushrooms to the baking sheet or skillet. Bake for 15 minutes or until marrow is soft and begins to separate from bones. In a small bowl, mix salt, olive oil, and lemon juice thoroughly, and then add the parsley and capers. Remove the bones and mushrooms from oven and place on large platter. To serve, slice the mushrooms into strips, scoop the marrow out of the bones and spread it on toast, and then sprinkle with the parsley and caper mixture.

BLOOD

No fewer than thirty dishes worldwide use blood in the cookery in one form or another. Only one is included here—black pudding—while blood sausage is included in the sausage section of this book. If you're so inclined, you can check into the uses of blood in creating other unique meals. Black pudding has long been a staple of Irish and British households, while blood sausage has a worldwide history.

BLACK PUDDING

2½ teaspoons salt, divided

4 cups fresh pork blood

1½ cups steel-cut oats

2 cups finely diced pork fat

1 large yellow onion, finely chopped

1 cup milk

1½ teaspoons ground black pepper

1 teaspoon ground allspice

Preheat the oven to 325°F and grease two glass loaf pans. Stir 1 teaspoon of salt into the blood. Bring 2½ cups of water to a boil in a medium saucepan and stir in the oats. Simmer, stirring occasionally, for 15 minutes, until just tender but not mushy. Pour the blood through a fine sieve into a large bowl to remove any lumps. Stir in the fat, onion, milk, pepper, allspice, and remaining 1½ teaspoons salt. Add the oatmeal and mix to combine. Divide the mixture between the loaf pans, cover with foil, and bake for 1 hour, until firm. Cool completely. Seal in plastic wrap and freeze, or store in refrigerator for up to 1 week. To serve, cut a ½-inch-thick slice off the loaf. Fry in butter or oil until the edges are slightly crispy and browned.

PIG TAIL AND EARS

Try using the tail and ears for crispy treats, much like bacon.

ROASTED PIG TAIL

With only one tail to work with per pig, you may have to go to a market to acquire more.

SAUTÉED PIG EARS

2 pig ears, cleaned

1 cup olive oil

1 teaspoon paprika

1 teaspoon salt

Cook the ears first by placing in saucepan and covering in water. Boil for 2 hours, topping off with water as needed. Remove any foam that surfaces. Then reduce the heat and simmer until the ears are soft enough for a fork to pass through. In a large frying pan, heat olive oil to shimmering. Slice the ears in ½-inch-wide strips and cook until crisp. Remove and cool. Sprinkle with paprika and salt and serve.

ROASTED PIG TAIL

1 medium onion, chopped

1 carrot, chopped

2 pounds pig tails, cleaned

3 cups red wine

1 tablespoon crushed dried bay leaves

1 tablespoon dried parsley flakes

1 tablespoon dried thyme

1 tablespoon whole peppercorns

1 teaspoon salt

Preheat the oven to 325°F. In a casserole dish, create a bed of the chopped onion and carrot and the place pig tails on top. Pour the wine over. Mix the bay leaves, parsley, thyme, peppercorns, and salt together in a small bowl and sprinkle over the top. Cover and bake for 3 hours. Remove, cool, and serve with crusted bread.

PIG FEET

There are many recipes for using pig feet. The following are only a few that can help you create interesting and unusual dishes.

BOILED PIG FEET

4 pig feet	1½ tablespoons salt

Scrape feet, wash thoroughly, and tie each separately in a piece of cheesecloth. Cover with boiling water and add salt. Heat to boiling, reduce heat, and simmer 6 hours. Cool in the water. When cold, drain, but do not remove cloth. Chill. Use for broiling, frying, and pickling.

Broiled Pigs' Feet—Split feet, sprinkle with salt, pepper, and flour, and broil for 10 minutes. Season with butter, salt, and pepper.

Fried Pigs' Feet—Split feet and season with salt, pepper, and lemon juice. Dip into beaten egg, then into bread crumbs, and fry in hot, deep fat (375ºF) for 5 minutes.

PIG KNUCKLES AND SAUERKRAUT

3 teaspoons salt	1 quart sauerkraut
4 pig knuckles	

Bring 2 quarts of water to a boil and stir in 3 teaspoons of salt. Add the whole knuckles and cover and simmer until the meat is tender, about 2½ to 3 hours. Twenty minutes before serving, pour off most of the water and add sauerkraut. Heat thoroughly. Serve the meat on a bed of sauerkraut.

PICKLED PIG FEET OR HOCKS

4 boiled pig feet or hocks

1 quart white distilled vinegar

4 fresh bay leaves

1 tablespoon whole cloves

1 tablespoon broken
   cinnamon stick chunks

¼ cup salt

2 teaspoons ground black pepper

1 large onion, cut into eighths

Clean the feet carefully, then place in a pot and cover with at least 2 quarts of hot water. Simmer for 1 hour or until the meat separates from the bones, then remove the meat carefully with a skimmer. Place in a crock or jar, taking out the large bones, skin, and most of the fat. Reserve the cooking liquid. In a nonreactive saucepan, heat the vinegar, bay leaves, cloves, cinnamon, salt, pepper, and onion. Simmer slowly for 45 minutes, but do not let boil at any time. Skim the fat from the top of the reserved cooking liquid and discard. Measure 1 quart of the liquid and add it to the vinegar mixture. Strain the liquid through a sieve and pour it over the meat. Seal the crock or jar and let stand in the refrigerator overnight and up to 2 days, depending on preference. Skim off any cooled fat from the top before serving.

PIG INTESTINES

Pig intestines will need intensive cleaning to remove any pungent odors and tastes before they are edible. The cleaning isn't impossible but is more difficult than with many other pig parts.

PIG INTESTINES

4 pounds pork intestines, cleaned

2 medium onions, peeled and halved

1 green pepper, sliced

1 celery stalk, chopped

2 garlic cloves, peeled

1 cup white vinegar

¼ cup lemon juice

2 tablespoons salt

2 tablespoons ground black pepper

In a large pot, place the cleaned intestines, onions, green pepper, celery, and garlic cloves in 4 quarts water. Add the vinegar, lemon juice, salt, and pepper and bring to boil. Simmer for 2½ hours or until intestines are soft. Remove and serve. Season to taste.

PIG SNOUT AND LIPS

The pig's lips can be pan-fried or used along with the snout in stir-fries and soups.

PIG SNOUT AND LIPS

1 pound pig snout and lips

3 tablespoons olive oil

1 tablespoon ground ginger

5 cloves garlic, minced

1 large onion, minced

2 tablespoons soy sauce

2 tablespoons sugar

1 teaspoon ground cinnamon

1 cup white wine

3 cups chicken broth

Slice the snout and lips into ¼-inch-thick strips. In large kettle, bring 6 cups of water to a boil and add the strips. Reduce the heat immediately and simmer for 1 hour. Skim the surface of any film or oil deposits. Drain the snout and lips and set aside. Heat olive oil in a medium skillet over medium heat. Add the ginger, garlic, and onion and sauté for 10 minutes. Add the strips, soy sauce, sugar, and cinnamon, and stir. Pour in the white wine and broth, stir and cover. Simmer for 1 hour or until the strips are fork tender. Remove and serve with vegetables.

PORK SKIN

The skin of the pig is often called the pork rind, and when fried or roasted, it is typically referred to as pork scratchings or pork cracklings. The rind is sometimes used in sausage making to help improve consistency. The tough skin of a pig can be made edible by a two-step process of rendering and drying it, and then frying what's left.

SPICED PORK SCRATCHINGS

½ teaspoon whole fennel seeds

½ teaspoon cumin seed

¼ teaspoon paprika

1½ tablespoons sea salt, divided

1 pound pork rind, with ½-inch fat

Toast the whole fennel and cumin seeds in a dry skillet over medium heat until fragrant, and then grind them together with paprika. Mix in ¾ tablespoon of salt. Preheat the oven to 425ºF. Cut the rind into strips 2 inches wide and 3 inches long. Rub the rind with the remaining ¾ tablespoon of salt and let rest for 20 minutes. Put the pieces on a rack in a roasting tray without touching each other. Roast in the oven for 20 to 25 minutes. Turn the roasting tray around every 5 minutes to make sure the rind doesn't burn. When the scratchings are bubbly and crisp, they are ready. Remove and place in a heat-resistant bowl. Mix in the spices and stir to coat evenly. Serve or store them in an airtight container for 2 to 3 days.

HEADCHEESE

One alternative for using the pig's head is to make headcheese. This in not cheese derived from milk but a meat jelly that can be made from a pig head. The eyes, ears, and brains are removed before the head is placed in a large pot or kettle and slowly boiled for 4 or 5 hours. Herbs such as bay leaves and vegetables such as carrots and onions are usually added to enhance the flavor, and sometimes the hocks and knuckles are added as well. Any meat scraps that have been left over from trimmings that you don't want to use for sausage, or that can be dedicated to this dish, can also be added. Gristly parts that offer no other alternative use and would benefit from long stewing can be added to this mix.

To begin, you should split the skull in half and remove the brains. Also remove both eyes and ears. Opening the skull bone will help in boiling it thoroughly. Set the brains aside, but keep them cool or chilled in a refrigerator, or freeze them for later use.

Place the head in a large pot or kettle, add water, and bring to a slow boil for 4 to 5 hours.

You want the head completely submerged so the size of the pot or kettle will be determined by the size of the head. Splitting the head in half will allow you the option of boiling one side at a time, which may then require a smaller pot or kettle. The process will be the same, only it will double the time required to finish it.

After the slow boil is finished, remove all pieces and place them in a large, rimmed cooking tray. Allow to drain as you scrape the skin and meat off the skull. When scraped clean, move the skull bone off to the side and start to chop the meat into diced or large coarse pieces.

In a large loaf cooking dish, layer the cut meat pieces with the herbs and vegetables that were in the boiling water. Then add the cooling liquid to cover all the loaf contents.

The head and meat scraps you boil will have enough connective tissue to create a natural gelatin as the water boils off. This will be used to help bind the loaf together as it cools.

When you have finished filling your loaf dish, allow it to set in a cool or cold temperature overnight to solidify. It will set into a jelly that can then be sliced and served cold.

PIG BLADDER

After rinsing the bladder and allowing it to sit in a salt brine for a minimum of 12 hours, thoroughly clean it by rinsing and scrubbing the insides before adding any ingredients.

After mixing and stuffing the contents into the bladder, it should be stitched shut on both open ends with cooking thread. You can poach it in boiling water. The insides will not come in contact with the water, and the juices from the meat will stay inside the bladder and make the stuffing very moist.

PIG BLADDER

1 pig bladder, brined and cleaned

8 ounces rolled oats

1 pound pork trimmings and fat

2 onions, diced fine

1 tablespoon salt

1 teaspoon ground black pepper

1 teaspoon ground dried coriander

1 teaspoon mace

1 teaspoon ground nutmeg

2 cups nonchlorinated water

Kettle of water to submerge bladder

Rinse the bladder in clean, cold water and set aside. Cook the oats according to package instructions. Dice the pork trimmings and fat into ⅛-inch cubes. Then mix onions, oatmeal, salt, pepper, coriander, mace, and nutmeg thoroughly together in bowl. Add water to moisten the mixture to a soft, crumbly consistency. Stitch one end of bladder shut with cooking thread. Spoon the mixture into the bladder and fill three-quarters full. Stitch the open end shut. Heat a pot of water to boiling and add the bladder. Reduce to a simmer and cook for 3 hours without a lid, adding water as needed to keep the bladder submerged. Remove and place on large serving platter. The cladder should be extended (like a football). To serve, cut open the bladder and spoon out the filling. Serve with mashed potatoes and red wine.

PIG UTERUS

The pig's uterus can be used in stir-fry dishes. Try the following.

STIR-FRY

2 tablespoons olive oil

1 pound pork tenderloin,
cubed into 1-inch pieces

1 pig uterus, sliced into 1-inch rolls

1 teaspoon red curry powder

1 teaspoon salt

1 teaspoon ground black pepper

¼ cup whole milk

1 tablespoon fish sauce

1 cup green whole peas

2 teaspoons chopped garlic

3 cups portabello mushrooms, cubed

¾ cup sliced green onions

2 lemon wedges

Cooked rice for serving

Heat oil in a wok or large skillet over medium-high heat. Sprinkle the pork and uterus evenly with curry powder, salt, and black pepper. Mix the milk and fish sauce together in a small bowl and set aside. Add the pork tenderloin and uterus pieces, peas, garlic, and mushrooms to the hot wok. Stir together and cook for 3 to 4 minutes. Add the milk and fish sauce and stir well. Stir in the onions. Cook until thoroughly heated. Remove from heat and squeeze the juice from the lemon wedges over before serving with rice and red wine.

HOME STORAGE OF FRESH PORK

Product	Refrigerator 40°F	Freezer 0°F
Fresh pork roast, steaks, chops, or ribs	3 to 5 days	4 to 6 months
Fresh pork liver or variety meats	1 to 2 days	3 to 4 months
Home-cooked pork; soups, stews, or casseroles	3 to 4 days	2 to 3 months
Store-cooked convenience meats	1 to 2 days	2 to 3 months
Frozen dinners & entrees	Keep frozen before cooking	3 to 4 months
Canned pork products in pantry	2 to 5 years in pantry; 3 to 4 days after opening	2 to 3 months

Source: USDA Food and Inspection Service

SAUSAGE STORAGE

All sausage, except for dry sausage, is perishable and must be kept refrigerated unless used immediately. The following storage times should be followed for maximum quality and safety.

Type of Sausage	Refrigerator— unopened	Refrigerator— after opening	Freezer
Fresh sausage, uncooked	1 to 2 days	1 to 2 days	1 to 2 months
Fresh sausage, after cooking at home	N/A	3 to 4 days	2 to 3 months
Hard/dry sausage, whole	6 weeks	3 weeks	1 to 2 months
Hot dogs and other cooked sausage	2 weeks	7 days	1 to 2 months
Lunchmeats	2 weeks	3 to 5 days	1 to 2 months
Summer sausage (semidry)	3 months	3 weeks	1 to 2 months

Source: USDA Food Safety and Inspection Service, 2013

RENDERING PORK LARD

The same process is used for rendering the two types of pork fat: back fat and leaf fat. Depending on the amount of fat you plan to render, you should allow for a time period of 3 to 8 hours. This will also depend on how much fat you process at one time. You can render all the fat at once or over several days, if you choose. But keep the fat you don't use right away either chilled or frozen until you do. In fact, lard is easiest to work with when it is frozen or at least well chilled.

Equipment for Rendering Fat

- Knife and cutting board

- Slow cooker, skillet, or kettle

- Wood cooking spoon

- Ladle

- Cheesecloth or fine sieve

- Wide-mouth glass canning jars with new lids

- Long-sleeve oven gloves

- Protective eyewear

First, a few safety rules. Although children should be part of your butchering process so they can learn and appreciate where their meat comes from, having them around while cooking fat can be dangerous. Keep young children away from your knives and stove once you begin your processing. Spitting fat or one accidental spillage of hot fat can cause severe burns or life-threatening injuries. You will need to focus on the process, and having children around may cause distractions. Keeping them away during the cooking is the best and safest policy.

But it's not only children who can be injured. You will be the one on the front line and working with hot fat, so you also need to take precautions. Use protective eyewear (no, it won't make you look silly) and oven gloves that have long sleeves to protect your forearms from spattering fat. Also, don't forget your legs and feet. Wearing long pants and shoes that completely cover the tops of your feet will be added protection from any drops of hot fat.

Now we're ready to start.

The Rendering Process

As a rule, 1 pound of unrendered pork fat will yield about 1 pint of rendered lard. So, if you have 20 pounds of fat to process, you will get roughly 20 pints or about 2½ gallons of lard. Here's how to start processing it:

Begin by cutting the fat into ½-inch cubes. This will allow for more surface area and allow each piece to be heated evenly.

Once you have a sufficient amount cut up—this will be determined by the size of your slow cooker, skillet, or kettle—you can place the cubed fat in it.

Add a ½ cup of water or enough to cover the bottom of the unit before you turn on the heat. The reason for the water, which will evaporate during the heating process, is to help transfer the heat from the stove into the cold fat without scorching or burning it. Metal skillet pans or a kettle will transfer heat from the stove coils to the fat rapidly. Your goal is to get the fat as hot as possible as quickly as possible without burning it. Lard has a rather low smoking temperature, smokes rapidly, and produces an irritating smoke. Like all animal fats, lard absorbs strong odors from foods.

Once the fat on the bottom begins to melt, it will transfer the heat and replace the function of the water. Keeping a lid on the skillet, kettle, or slow cooker during the first 10 minutes will trap the heat in and help raise the initial temperature quickly. It is generally best to begin with medium heat regardless of whether you use a skillet, kettle, or slow cooker.

Once the fat has started to liquefy, you can remove the lid to allow steam or moisture to evaporate. You want the fat to simmer, not boil, so monitor the fat and temperature closely.

Never leave your cooking fat unattended. This is one reason to block out a set amount of time and dedicate it to this task. Should fat come into contact with a stove's coils for any reason, it could ignite into a grease fire, which can have disastrous consequences.

As the fat cooks down, the volume decreases. When the mixture is about half liquid and half solid, it is time for you to remove some of the liquid to allow the remaining fat pieces to cook down more easily.

To separate the solids from the liquid, you can use a slotted ladle or spoon, a fine mesh colander or strainer, or cheesecloth. You need a heat-resistant bowl in which to collect the liquid lard.

Strain the pieces from the liquid and place them in another heat-resistant bowl. Pour the liquid through the strainer or cheesecloth to collect any solid pieces and bits that are not fat.

After draining the liquid fat, replace the large fat pieces back into the pan, skillet, or pot to allow them to heat and liquefy as the rendering process continues. You can add more at this stage or start later with a fresh batch of fat cubes. As the pieces melt, repeat the draining process, but make sure the bowl has enough room to hold what you pour. After the first batch is finished, you can start a second, if you've allowed time for it.

The solid bits and pieces that you've strained or filtered out are minute pieces of tissue that had helped to bind the fat together in the pig as well as some meat that was trimmed along with the fat when cutting up the carcass. This can be set aside and used for cracklings or fed to your chickens or large pets.

Once you have completed the process of rendering the fat, you should allow the liquid to cool before pouring it into canning jars. These jars are adaptable to high-heat temperatures if the glass is raised in temperature incrementally. Pouring boiling fat into a cold glass jar is too extreme a temperature rise too quickly and likely will compromise the jar's integrity, either shattering or cracking it. Allowing the fat to cool will reduce the differences in the two temperatures and make it safer to pour.

Using wide-mouth jars will allow you to use a clean funnel to help pour the liquid in it. Also, it will be easier to spoon out the solidified lard for use if the mouth is wider.

When it's hot, lard is clear and usually has a slightly yellow glow. But it will turn snow white as it cools in your refrigerator.

Naturally rendered lard has a long shelf life if kept in a cool, dry place out of sunlight. In well-sealed jars, it can be kept for extended periods. However, if you don't use it quickly, it is better to refrigerate it until it's used up. Rendered lard can be kept in your freezer almost indefinitely.

Fill the jars about three-quarters full with liquid fat. Don't fill it completely to the top. Allow it to cool completely and then seal with a lid and screw on the top ring. By letting it cool completely before sealing, you will allow heat and any moisture to escape without building up any pressure inside the jar.

If you plan to freeze lard in jars, remember to allow enough of an empty space at the top so there is room for possible expansion as the fat freezes. If there is not enough room, any expansion may crack the jar. This is not disastrous because the lard will still be good. But if it happens, be sure to inspect the lard for any possible glass shards once you begin to use it.

After you have finished rendering all the fat you have available, you will be able to use it for cooking and baking, and your pig will have helped.

Chapter 9

SMOKING AND CURING PORK

Smoking and curing are two preservation methods you can use for pork. Both processes involve drying the meat, which will help inhibit bacterial growth. This makes your pork cuts viable for long-term storage. Curing meat in your home can be done safely and effectively. You can smoke almost any part of your pig carcass, but in particular the bacon, ham, pork shoulders, ribs, hocks, and jowls to enhance their flavor.

Smoking and curing pork will extend its shelf life and adds a flavor particular to the method used. You can make sausages and patties and use smoke to add another layer of flavor to them. Using proper smoking equipment is essential, and while curing pork can be done with indoor processes such as a dry rub, brine submersion, or pickling with an acidic base, smoking will need to be done outdoors or in a well-ventilated area such as a garage or shed.

HEALTH CONCERNS FROM EATING SMOKED PORK

While there may be legitimate health concerns regarding the consumption of large quantities of smoked pork or other meat products, this should not deter you from using them in moderation. Most of these health issues are a result of the smoke, which contains coal tars and polycyclic aromatic hydrocarbons (PAHs) that are considered carcinogenic. You may want to use your smoked meats as special treats rather than for daily meals.

Sodium Nitrite and Nitrate Concerns

Many recipes that have been handed down through the years called for saltpeter, or potassium nitrate. Most sausage supply companies no longer sell saltpeter, but you will find other commercial products that accomplish similar results, such as Morton Salt's Tender Quick mix, which is a fast cure containing 0.5 percent sodium nitrate and 0.5 percent sodium nitrite and is used in some recipes at the rate of 1 teaspoon per pound of meat.

The University of Minnesota published findings in 1992 that a fatal dose of potassium nitrate, or saltpeter, for adults is in the range of 30 to 35 grams (slightly more than 1 ounce) consumed in a single dose. The fatal dose of sodium nitrite is in the range of 22 to 23 milligrams per kilogram of body weight. Nitrates are found in vegetables such as spinach, beets, radishes, celery, onions, and cabbages, so they are not uncommon substances.

The concerns of consuming too much nitrates or nitrites in meat center on the quantity eaten rather than its inclusion as a preservative. The Minnesota report concluded that nitrite as it is used in meat such as sausages is considered safe because the known benefits outweigh the potential risks. You can stay with fresh sausages if you are concerned about limiting nitrites and nitrates in your diet.

Fermento is a commercially available dairy-based product made from cultured whey protein and skim milk. It is used to produce a tangy taste in semidry sausages, such as some summer sausages and Thuringer sausage. The "tang" found in fermented, dry-cured meat is due to a decrease in pH as the lactic acid builds up. This product mimics that taste, as does citric acid. However, citric acid is not lactic acid and will not yield the same flavor. The key to having a tangy-flavored sausage is proper fermentation produced by specific bacteria that are added to the meat as a starter culture. You will have more control over this flavor by adding the recommended amounts.

The recommended level of use is 3 percent, or about 1 ounce per pound of meat. It is possible to double this percentage to produce a more tangy taste, but if you exceed 6 percent, the sausage likely will become mushy. Fermento does not need to be refrigerated and quickens the fermentation process. Instead of several days that is often required for starter cultures to start fermentation, this product can be added and the fermentation will take only hours before you can begin smoking the meat.

TWO TYPES OF SMOKING

There are two forms of smoking meats: hot smoking and cold smoking, and they are identified by the temperatures used with them. These temperatures will be applied to different meats in several ways, always keeping in mind the critical internal temperature that needs to be reached to make the meat safe to eat. These internal temperatures will vary slightly between animal and fowl species, such as pork needing to reach an internal temperature of 160°F to be considered safe, while poultry needs 165°F.

Hot smoking means to cook the meat at or above 150°F in a smoking unit. Pork sausages, which are made from smaller meat particles and often less dense in texture than whole cuts, are recommended to be hot smoked at 180°F because of the increased exposure the meat particles have from being ground up, along with a higher fat content. For whole cuts, the recommended temperature is 200°F, allowing for slow cooking and maximum smoke. If unsure of your equipment or your smoking unit has a heat control, hot smoke all recipes at 200°F for safety, unless specified differently.

Cold smoking refers to a temperature of less than 100°F and is usually difficult to achieve without proper equipment. If any recipe calls for cold smoking, it will assume you have a unit that can stay below 100°F indefinitely. This is hard to do consistently and is not a recommended practice, especially when you are just beginning a smoking career. If you pursue cold smoking, you will need to make certain the temperature doesn't rise above 95°F to 100°F to be safe. You should assume that any recipes appearing in this book that require smoking refer to a hot smoking method.

CURES

If you plan to make smoked, cooked, or dry sausages, you will need to use a *cure*. A cure, or curing solution, is the addition of salt, sodium, or potassium nitrates that inhibit and/or prevent the growth of the botulism bacteria. Nitrites are made from the natural breakdown of either sodium or potassium nitrate. Older generations used saltpeter, a strong form of nitrate (sodium or potassium) to cure their meats. Better alternatives are available today, and these will be discussed here.

Clostridium botulinum is the bacteria that causes botulism, a potent and deadly form of food poisoning. The spores thrive in meat environments with temperatures between 40°F and 140°F, and with moist, low oxygen conditions. This is exactly the environment we provide in sausage smokers, dry sausages, and fresh pork held at room temperature.

This, then, is the main reason for using a cure product with processing meat. At this time, there is no known substitute for nitrite in curing meat and sausages. The benefits of using it far outweigh any health risks that may be associated with it. You can go without using nitrites if cooking fresh pork right after butchering the pig, but sooner or later you will need to consider how best to preserve the rest you can't eat right away.

The botulism bacteria are present in many soil conditions, vegetables, and other foods we consume. So, how real is the danger of it? If you consume it, it is a very real danger and it comes with a high risk of dying or encountering severe nerve damage. Yet it's not likely you will ever experience its effects because commercially available food products are strictly regulated and monitored. Most botulism cases occurring in the United States are a result of improper home canning. Botulism spores are hard to kill but aren't harmful except, potentially, to infants. The spores in the soil and vegetables typically are not found in sufficient quantities to be deadly to humans. However, when these bacteria are allowed to grow in an oxygen-free (anaerobic), nonacidic environment between 40°F and 140°F, they will multiply rapidly and start producing the deadly toxin.

Curing Salts

To inhibit the botulism spores and their growth, a curing salt of some form *must be used* in any dry-cured sausages. There are no exceptions.

Sodium nitrite, often referred to as a pink salt because of its color, prevents these bacteria from growing. Sodium nitrate, for example, will act as a sort of time-release capsule form of sodium nitrite and must be used in all dry-cured sausages cured for long periods, such as salamis, which may be cold-smoked and then dried for weeks.

Be aware that these cures themselves can be dangerous if ingested, such as accidentally licking your finger that may be covered with these salts. There is a reason for curing salts to appear in recipes, and you should always use them in the proportions stated in the recipe. Keep them out of the reach of children!

While you need to take precautions using curing salts, they are beneficial and have three main functions: killing a range of bacteria, especially those responsible for botulism; preserving the pink color we associate with meats; and adding a tangy flavor to the meat.

Nitrates actually do nothing beneficial to food until they convert to nitrite. Potassium nitrate (saltpeter) was used until the 1970s, when it was largely discontinued because it was too inconsistent to be safe. Sodium nitrate is now manufactured and sold under the commercial brand names of InstaCure #2 and DQ Curing Salt #2.

For purposes of discussion rather than recommendation, three commercially available brand-name cures are frequently used: Prague Powder #1 and #2, Morton Tender Quick, and InstaCure #1 and #2. Another includes tinted curing mix (TCM), which is also referred to as Prague powder or pink salt.

Regardless of the name, their composition is the same: 93.75 percent salt and 6.25 percent nitrite. Always use them based on the directions given by the supplier as one brand may have a higher concentration of sodium nitrite than another.

As an example, referring to the above products, the Prague Powder #1 and #2 are used for different products; #1 is for all cured meats and sausages, except for kinds like salami, and #2 is used for dried meat and sausages. Both are used in very small quantities, but, again, you must follow the supplier's directions exactly. Morton Tender Quick contains both sodium nitrite and sodium nitrate. It has a lower nitrite-to-nitrate concentration (0.5 percent of each) and much more salt than the other cures.

This makes the Morton product good as a rub or in a brine, but it has a more limited use in sausage making because, with the extra salt, it can get very salty before the correct amount of cure is reached. InstaCure #1 and #2 are similar to the Prague powder and can work very well with any sausage making or meat curing. You should do your own research before beginning on sausage making to make the decisions that will affect your resulting products.

The bottom line, if not underlined then in big, bold, letters, is that you need to use a cure if you want safe smoked, cooked, or dried sausage. Sodium nitrate, and the sodium nitrite it produces, is a safe product for curing meats and sausages.

Dry Cures

A dry cure is one in which a salt mixture is rubbed over the meat or the meat is rolled in it to cover it completely. Most salt referred to is sodium chloride and appears as such in the recipes in this book. When a cure is listed, it refers to salts that have nitrite in them and sometimes nitrates. A dry cure may also contain sugar.

A generic dry cure ratio of salt to sugar is 2:1, plus 10 percent of their combined weight of cure. For example, 1 ounce of pink salt is enough

Basic Pork Cure Recipe

1 pound salt

8 ounces sugar

2 ounces (10 teaspoons) pink salt

Mix all ingredients thoroughly. Store in a sealed, nonmetallic container.

for 25 pounds of meat. Salt is important as an active ingredient, and sugar helps mitigate the harshness of the salt, such as adding brown sugar or a maple syrup to curing salty bacon.

Using acid in the dry-cure process is an important part. Many professionals use a live culture that feeds on the sugar in the sausage mixture and releases lactic acid. This reduces the pH level and helps prevent bacterial growth. One commercially available product is Bactoferm F-RM-52. Live cultures are kept frozen until use when they are rehydrated. If using this kind of product, always use nonchlorinated or distilled water to prevent the chlorine from killing the live cultures. Don't scrimp on using such a culture. While it is not needed in great amounts, you still must use enough, even if you overdo it, to ensure that a sufficient amount of live culture gets into the sausage. This product is completely safe, and adding too much will not be harmful to you.

SMOKING

Smoking pork, or any meat, accomplishes three objectives:

- It gives the meat a unique flavor, depending on the type of wood used.

- It helps to lower the moisture content within the meat, which reduces the chance for bacterial growth.

- It adds color to the surface of the pork cut.

Three factors affect the amount of time the meat needs to be cured: the density of the meat cut, such as whether it is a thick ham or small sausage patty; the amount of smoke generated within the smoking unit; and the ability of the meat surface to absorb smoke.

The density of the pork cut you want to smoke will affect the time required to adequately complete the process. This is because it will take longer for the smoke and heat to penetrate a thicker piece than a smaller piece, such as a sausage link or a flat bacon slab.

The length of time that the smoke fills the chamber will affect the amount of smoke deposited on the surface of the meat. Variations in smoke density will also affect how much the smoke components adhere to the surface.

The meat surface itself will also affect how the smoke is absorbed. Temperature control at this stage will be important because if the meat surface gets too hot, too quickly it will deter the smoke from attaching to it because the surface has dried too fast. To successfully smoke your pork, and to get a satisfying result, the surface needs to be slightly moist so that it can attract the smoke particles. Smoke will not adhere to dry surfaces, although it will blacken it in color. You will need to dry the surface enough to remove excess moisture while still leaving enough moisture to absorb the smoke.

WOOD TYPES FOR SMOKING

Different woods will create subtle, but different, flavors, depending on which you use. Natural wood smoke is generally produced from hardwood sawdust, wood chips, or small logs.

You can use a variety of different hardwoods for smoking. The most popular is hickory, although other hardwoods, such as oak, maple, ash, mesquite, cherry, apple, and other fruit woods, can be used.

Selecting the type of wood to use for smoking pork is more a matter of personal choice than anything. One standard rule applies, however: the best woods for smoking are dried (cured) hardwoods with a low sap flow. Avoid using pine or other coniferous trees because of their high tar content, which will create a bitter flavor on the meat.

WOODS FOR SMOKING

Mild (best for foods not heavily seasoned or sauced)
Alder
Apple
Cherry
Grape
Maple
Mulberry
Orange
Peach

Strong (best for strong-flavored foods with spice or sauce)
Hickory (good for pork)
Mesquite
Oak
Pecan
Walnut

Woods can be divided into two basic groups that are based on whether they yield a mild or strong flavor, rather than tree species. For mild smoke flavors, use alder, apple, cherry, maple, orange, or peach woods. For stronger flavors, use hickory, oak, mesquite, pecan, and walnut.

WOOD CONSIDERATIONS

Natural wood smoke contains three major components: solids, such as ash and tar; air and combustion gases; and acids, carbonyls, phenolics, and polycyclic aromatic hydrocarbons (PAHs).

Research has shown that the ash and tar and the gases do not contribute very much to the flavor, aroma, or preservative properties of smoked products, while the phenolics have been identified as the primary source for them. The carbonyls are the source of color, typically the amber brown, generated from the smoking process.

If you use natural wood for smoking, it is important to use only air-dried woods and never use moldy woods that may contain toxins, have paint on them, or have been treated. Many of the woods you use can be purchased at specialty stores, outdoor outlets, or cut and dried by yourself.

The dry wood used for smoking usually needs to be soaked in water for a short time prior to being used in a smoker. This will prevent it from burning. Although burning wood will create some smoke, it won't be enough for your purposes. The idea is to create smoke, not a flame, and to add flavor rather than heat—although some heat is a partial requirement for successfully smoking pork. But more on this later.

CURING

Cured ham or cured bacon are terms that are familiar with many people. They conjure up smells and tastes for those who have experienced them. For those who have not, there are pork products that you will be able to create yourself with the help of this book. The curing process will be explained and you will be able to use it with a variety of pig parts.

Curing is the chemical or physical processing of meat to allow it to be safely edible for a long period of time. This process includes the use of salt and other preserving agents that kill, retard, or inhibit the production of spoilage bacteria.

Salt is the essential ingredient in any successful curing process. It draws moisture from the muscle cell by osmosis. This process distributes the salt through the muscle tissue. It checks the action of bacteria, which need a moist environment to propagate. Without this moisture, the bacteria cannot grow. Unless spoilage has already occurred within the tissue before it is cured, any bacteria present will be in insufficient quantities to become harmful. This is the main reason to keep fresh meat chilled between the times you butcher and cut up the carcass and when you process or package it.

The amount of salt you use is also a consideration. Too little salt used in the curing process can allow those bacteria that are able to grow in the presence of salt to get an upper hand by not being adequately checked. From this, spoilage can follow. On the other hand, if too much salt is used, the meat can become hard, dry, and taste overly salty.

Large portions of pork, such as hams and shoulders, generally will take a longer curing time than smaller pieces. It takes more time to allow the salts or brine to reach sufficient concentration in the tissues to protect the centers of these larger cuts. This likely will mean that you will need a storage space dedicated to this purpose, as well as one free from insects, pets, and children while the curing processes work their way to their intended conclusion.

SMOKING UNITS

You can use a variety of smoking units. They can range from home grills with covers to substantial upright units that sit in your backyard. They can be electric or fully powered by wood. Or, you can construct a smokehouse for your own use. The amount of meat and the size of the cuts will largely determine the type of smoking unit needed. Also your budget and the space available for a unit may be considerations.

You can use traditional smoking units, such as smokehouses or metal chambers specifically designed for smoking meats, that accomplish two things at once. They provide a proper temperature to kill harmful pathogens, and they produce a pleasing smoky flavor.

Units made for home use include vertical electric water smokers, insulated variable-temperature smokers, electric smokers, stovetop smokers, covered grills, and charcoal-fired smokers. Understanding their advantages and limitations may help you decide which is best for you. The following are just brief descriptions of a few types of smokers, but you should research all the models that are commercially available to determine which one will work best for you. Their prices range from modest to expensive, and this may give some indication of their durability. Some are stationary, while others may be set on rollers for easier movement. They may be rectangular or round, and the number of racks may increase with larger units. Several types of digitally controlled smoker models are available and are popular because they allow you to easily monitor the temperature and time.

One concern about smokers, depending on the model used, is the potential loss of heat caused by opening a door to add water to a pan or to replenish wood chips, pellets, or logs. Models are available that have external wood chip or pellet loaders so the unit doesn't need to be opened. Some smokers have a tray that can be pulled out, have fresh chips or pellets added to it, and be pushed back into the unit without opening the door. This is an outdoor model not meant for indoor use.

Vertical electric water smokers are popular because they are generally the least expensive smokers on the market. The less costly models may not reach the high temperatures you need. The more expensive models, however, have better temperature control. These units have either a gas or electric heat source and typically have three components: a bottom heat source, a water pan that stores heat and regulates the internal temperature, and a smoking chamber. The biggest disadvantage is the loss of heat when the lid is opened. You can mitigate this by having a thermometer that can signal the temperature to an outside receiver.

An insulated variable-temperature smoker has good temperature control. This variety is becoming more popular with those who want to do home smoking. They are typically more expensive than other models but are easy to use and generally conform to the same dynamics as a vertical electric water smoker.

Electric smokers are another popular type because they are easy to use and don't take up a lot of space. The more expensive models typically have a rheostat that turns down the electricity flow to the coil, much like that found on an electric stove or hot plate, and they may have multiple settings ranging from low to high. Some of the more expensive electric smokers have thermostats that have a temperature probe inside the cooking chamber. The thermostat monitors the temperature and will raise it if it's too low or lower it if it's too high. This makes a unit with a thermostat better than one with a rheostat, but also makes the unit more expensive. One drawback to this type of unit is that it doesn't work well outdoors in cold weather.

Stovetop smokers have become available in recent years and may solve space concerns, but they cannot be used for very large pieces of pork. They will work well for sausages or other smaller size pieces that may be left over from processing the carcass. Stovetop smokers are stainless-steel units with an enclosed system that uses your stove's burners for heat to activate the flavored wood chips that are sprinkled across the inside bottom of the pan. The sausages are placed on a grill rack that is set above the base. The cover tightly seals in the heat and smoke.

Stovetop smokers work well in apartments or places where other smoking units can't be used. They are inexpensive, easy to use and clean, and will work with other meats as well. One drawback is their size. Most of these models range between 7 and 11 inches wide and 11 and 15 inches long, limiting the amount of pork or sausages they can hold at one time.

A covered grill and charcoal-fired smokers can be used to smoke pork, although it is more difficult to maintain an even temperature and smoke with them than with enclosed units. You will need to monitor the internal temperature and add wood chips or charcoal briquettes to maintain a proper temperature.

THERMOMETERS

You will need two types of thermometers to make sure the pork is smoked safely: one for the meat and one for the smoker. A thermometer is needed to monitor the air temperature in the smoker or grill to be sure the heat stays between 225°F and 300°F throughout the cooking process. Many of the new model smokers have built-in thermometers to help.

Using a food thermometer to determine the meat temperature is a good practice. Oven-safe thermometers can be inserted in the pork and remain there during smoking. Once the meat is removed from the smoker, you can use an instant-read thermometer to check the temperature. Again, the cooking time will depend on several factors, including the size of the pieces, their shape, the distance they are from the heat, the temperature of the coals, and the weather.

SMOKEHOUSES

If you are considering an annual butchering schedule, you may want to consider constructing a stationary smokehouse for long-term use. While these are more elaborate structures than the smoking units previously discussed, they will accommodate larger quantities of meats at one time and will last for many years. They have the advantage of making temperature control easier, and their tight construction and well-fitted ventilators can control airflow past the meat.

Any smokehouse you construct should have four features: a source of smoke, a place to hold smoke, a method to hold the meat in the smoke, and a draft regulator near the top or bottom. A smokehouse is a very slow oven in which the temperature does not exceed 200ºF. Even though you will use and maintain low temperatures, build your smokehouse in a safe location away from other buildings, particularly your home, and away from combustible materials. Be sure to check with local ordinances and fire codes before you begin any construction. You can get construction diagrams from many contractors or your county extension service.

While smokehouses are excellent for processing meats, they do not make a good storage area for smoke-finished meats. After your smoking process is complete, flies will eventually get in.

SMOKING FROZEN PORK

You can smoke pork that has been previously frozen. However, you must first thaw it out completely before smoking it. Because smoking uses low temperatures to cook food, the meat will take too long to thaw in the smoker. This will allow it to linger in the danger zone mentioned earlier of temperatures between 40ºF and 140ºF, where harmful bacteria can multiply.

Never thaw out pork at room temperature. Keep it cold in your refrigerator while the frozen pork is thawing. This is essential to keep harmful bacteria from growing while it is thawing. You can microwave the pork to thaw it more rapidly. But you then must smoke it immediately because some of the areas of the meat may begin to cook during the microwave thawing process.

You can also thaw the pork by wrapping it in an airtight package and submerging it in cold water. Then change the water every 30 minutes to maintain a temperature below 40ºF. When it is thawed, it must be cooked immediately.

BE SAFE

Depending on where you place your smoking unit, make sure there is adequate ventilation so that any escaping heat and smoke does not create air-quality problems, such as carbon monoxide in your home, shed, or apartment. Carbon monoxide is an invisible, odorless gas that can be produced by malfunctioning appliances, such as gas- or wood-burning stoves, fireplaces, and smokers. Carbon monoxide alarms are available, and you should have one installed inside your home if you use a smoker indoors.

SMOKING PORK

Any cut from the carcass can be smoked, and this section will guide you through the smoking processes for them. If you choose to smoke pork cuts, you should be aware of certain dynamics involved. This is due to the possible presence of *trichinae*, a small slender worm that may be present in the muscle. It is a parasite when

Cooking Temperature for Pork

Previous cooking guidelines called for a minimum internal temperature that was higher than 145ºF. The new recommendation reflects advances in food safety and the nutritional content of pork. Research shows that most common cuts of pork are 16 percent leaner than 20 years ago, and the saturated fat has dropped 27 percent. This drop in pork muscle fat content allows for a lower cooking temperature to reach the same safe degree of doneness that the higher temperature previously did.

in a larval stage in the voluntary muscles of humans and hogs. An infection occurs after the pig ingests the parasites. They burrow into the muscles and can cause muscle pain, fever, and other physical effects.

Not all pork will be infected by these parasites, whether you purchase your pork at a market or raise the animal yourself. Because these parasites are too small to be seen without using a microscope, you need to be cautious and take several steps to eliminate any potential problems.

First, cook all fresh pork to a minimum internal temperature of 145°F and allow for a 3-minute rest. During this rest time, its temperature remains constant or continues to rise, ensuring the destruction of any harmful germs. The internal tissue does not stop cooking at the exact moment you remove the meat from the heat source. The internal heat will continue to penetrate into the tissue until the heat source is removed. Once it is removed, there is no longer a heat penetration into the tissue, and the internal temperature will start to drop after about 3 minutes.

WHICH PARTS TO SMOKE

Almost every part of the pig carcass can be smoked. Some cuts are larger than others and will take more time to complete the smoking process, but all can be used. Bacon, hams, and shoulders are the cuts most often smoked. Jowls, ribs, and loins can be smoked too. Sausages can be smoked, and these are covered elsewhere in this book.

Bacon comes from the belly section of the carcass. If meat from other portions of the carcass is used, it may carry the name of where it came from, such as pork shoulder bacon. Pork bacon must be cooked before eating. Most bacon made from your pig carcass will be streaky bacon—the long narrow slices cut crosswise from the belly that contain veins of pink muscle layered within the white fat. These muscles and surrounding fat

hold the internal organs intact and protect them from outside injury. You will have trimmed the belly into rectangular or square shapes before slicing into strips. Although you may smoke and heat the bacon, it must be cooked before it is eaten.

Hams are popular for smoking either boneless or with the bone intact. A ham that has the center bone removed will take less time to heat and smoke than one in which the leg bone is still intact. It will take the heat longer to penetrate completely through to the bone and reach the critical 145°F internal temperature next to the bone. If smoking a ham, it is best to remove the skin and fat as the smoke will not penetrate into the meat if it is still on. Then when this outer layer of skin and fat is removed, all smoke flavor will be removed too.

Pork shoulders can be smoked, and as the name applies, they are located in the front part of the carcass. These will be large cuts and, like hams, will take longer to smoke and heat unless they are cut into smaller pieces.

Ribs, jowls, and loins are smaller cuts that can be smoked and will take less time to finish. The term *Canadian bacon* involves round slices of pink meat from the loin.

Try to cook pieces that are similar in size, as this will allow you to cook them at a specific temperature for an equal time and have a uniform result. Unevenly matched pieces may become overdone and too dry, or undercooked and unsafe.

SMOKING CONSIDERATIONS

The length of time that the smoke fills the chamber will largely determine the amount of smoke deposits on the surface of the meat. Variations in smoke density will also affect how much the smoke components adhere to the surface.

As a general rule, high smoking temperatures (110°F and above) with a light smoke will speed up the drying while lower temperatures (80°F to 110°F) with a dense smoke will intensify the smoky flavor in the meat.

Once the smoke cycle is completed, you can gradually increase the temperature inside the chamber to cook the meat. Don't increase the temperature too quickly or it will dry and overcook the surface before the required internal temperature is reached. By increasing the temperature in increments, you will be able to conduct the heat through the meat to minimize the difference between the surface and internal temperature. A long, slow cook will tenderize the meat to maximum effect.

SMOKED MAPLE BACON

¼ cup salt

2 teaspoons cure

¼ cup dark brown sugar

¼ cup maple syrup

1–5 pounds slab pork belly, skin on

Thoroughly mix salt, cure, and brown sugar in a nonmetallic container. Add the maple syrup and mix thoroughly. Rub the mixture over the entire surface of the pork belly. Place skin-side down in large container so the belly lies flat. Refrigerate for 7 days, turning it over every day, until the meat is firm to touch. Once firm, remove from brine, rinse thoroughly, and pat dry. Place on a rack set over a baking pan and dry in the refrigerator, uncovered, for 12 to 24 hours. Hot-smoke to an internal temperature of 160°F for 3 hours. Let cool until skin can be removed from fat, leaving as much fat on bacon as possible. (The skin can be used for cracklings or stock.) Let the bacon cool. Wrap in plastic, and refrigerate or freeze until ready to use.

SMOKED PORK HOCKS

1 gallon water

1½ cups salt

1 cup sugar

8 teaspoons cure

4 fresh pork hocks

Combine water, salt, sugar, and cure into a brine. Put in large pot and bring to a simmer. Stir until the salt and sugar are dissolved. Remove the brine from heat and let cool. Refrigerate until thoroughly chilled. Add the hocks to the brine and place a dish over them to keep them submerged. Refrigerate 3 days. Remove the hocks from brine and discard the brine (do not reuse). Rinse the hocks well and pat dry. Refrigerate on a rack set over a baking tray, uncovered, for 24 hours. Hot-smoke hocks to an internal temperature of 160ºF.

CANADIAN BACON

1 gallon water

1½ cups salt

1 cup sugar

8 teaspoons cure

3 cups chopped fresh sage

3 cups chopped fresh thyme

2 garlic cloves, peeled and crushed

4 pounds boneless pork loin, fat removed

In a pot large enough to hold the pork loin, combine the water, salt, sugar, cure, sage, thyme, and garlic, and bring to a simmer to dissolve the sugar and salt. Remove from heat and let cool to room temperature, then refrigerate until chilled. Place the pork loin in brine and place a weight on top to completely submerge the meat. Refrigerate for 48 hours. Remove the loin from the brine and discard the brine (do not reuse). Rinse the loin with cold water and pat dry. Place the loin on a rack over a baking tray and refrigerate for 24 hours. Hot-smoke the pork to an internal temperature of 160ºF for 2 to 3 hours, depending on taste. Then cover and refrigerate for up to 10 days.

Chapter 10

MORE PORK RECIPES

TIMETABLE FOR COOKING HAM

Cut	Weight in pounds	Minutes per pound	Minimum Internal Temperature & Rest Time
Smoked ham, cook before eating			
Whole, bone-in	10–14	18–20	145ºF and allow to rest for 3 minutes
Half, bone-in	5–7	22–25	"
Shank or butt portion, bone-in	3–4	35–40	"
Arm picnic shoulder, boneless	5–8	30–35	"
Shoulder roll (butt), boneless	2–4	35–40	"
Smoked ham, cooked			
Whole, bone-in	10–14	15–18	Reheat cooked hams packaged in USDA-inspected plants to 140ºF and all others to 165ºF.
Half, bone-in	5–7	18–24	
Arm picnic shoulder, boneless	5–8	25–30	
Canned ham, boneless	3–10	15–20	
Vacuum packed, boneless	6–12	10–15	
Spiral cut, whole or half	7–9	10–18	
Fresh Ham, uncooked			
Whole leg, bone-in	12–16	22–26	145ºF, and allow to rest for 3 minutes
Whole leg, boneless	10–14	22–26	
Half, bone-in	5–8	35–40	
Country Ham			

Whole or half: Soak 4 to 12 hours in refrigerator. Cover with water and boil 20 to 25 minutes per pound. Drain, glaze, and brown at 400ºF for 15 minutes.

Source: USDA Food Safety and Inspection Service, 2015

PORK COOKING TIMES AND TEMPERATURES

Cut	Thickness/Weight	Internal Temperature (followed by 3-minute rest)	Average Recommended Cooking Time (minutes/pound or total)
Roasting/Baking (unless otherwise noted, roast at 350°F in a shallow pan, uncovered)			
Ham, fully cooked	5–6 pounds	140°F	20 min. per pound
Pork belly (roast at 325°F + 450°F)	2 ½–3 pounds	Tender	45 min. per lb. at 325°F+15 min. browning at 450°F
Ribs			
Pork back	1½–2 lbs. per rack	Tender	1½–2 hours
Country-style	3–4 lbs.	Tender	1–1¼ hours
Spareribs (St. Louis–style)	3½–4 lbs. per rack		1½–2 hours
Roasts			
Fresh leg/uncured ham (bone-in)	16–17 lbs.	145–160°F	15 min. per lb.
	18–20 lbs.	145–160°F	13–14 min. per lb.
Fresh leg/uncured ham (boneless)	3–4 lbs.	160°F	30 min. per lb.
Shoulder (roast at 275°F)	3–6 lbs.	Tender	55–85 min. per lb.
Loin roast, boneless			
New York (top loin)	2 lbs.	145–160°F	26–28 min. per lb.
Pork roast	3–5 lbs.	145–160°F	20–25 min. per lb.
Sirloin pork roast	2 lbs.	145–160°F	26–28 min. per lb.
	3–5 lbs.	145–160°F	20–25 min. per lb.
Loin roast, bone-in			
Pork crown roast	10 lbs.	145–160°F	12–15 min. per lb.
Rack of pork	4–5 lbs.	145–160°F	25–40 min. per lb.
Sirloin pork roast	4–5 lbs.	145–160°F	25–40 min. per lb.
Stuffed pork loin chops	1¼–1½ inches	165°F	Varied, based on type of stuffing
Tenderloin (roast at 425°F)	1–1½ inches	145–160°F	20–35 min.
Whole pork loin (boneless)	8–10 lbs.	145–160° F	8–11 min. per lb.

Cut	Thickness/Weight	Internal Temperature (followed by 3-minute rest)	Average Recommended Cooking Time (minutes/pound or total)
Broiling (4–5 inches away from heat; turn halfway through cooking time) or Grilling (over direct, medium heat; turn once halfway through grilling)			
Blade pork steak	¾-inch	Tender	10–12 min.
Chops (boneless)			
New York (top loin pork chop)	¾ inches	145–160ºF	8–12 min.
	1½ inches	145–160ºF	12–22 min.
Ribeye (rib) pork chop	¾ inch	145–160ºF	8–12 min.
Sirloin pork chop	¾ inch	145–160ºF	8–12 min.
Chops (bone-in)			
Porterhouse (loin) pork chop	¾ inch	145–160ºF	8–12 min.
	1½ inches	145–160ºF	22–35 min.
Ribeye (rib) pork chop	¾ inch	145–160ºF	8–12 min.
Sirloin pork chop	¾ inch	145–160ºF	8–12 min.
Ground pork patties	½ inch	160ºF	8–12 min.
Ham steaks, bone-in	½ inch	140ºF	6 min.
Loin kabobs	1-inch cubes	Tender	8–10 min.
Tenderloin	1–1½ lbs.	145–160ºF	20–30 min.
Barbecuing (barbecue over indirect medium heat, about 325°F, unless otherwise noted)			
Blade (shoulder)	3–4 lbs.	Tender	45–75 min. per lb.
Pork steak	5–6 lbs.	Tender	30–45 min. per lb.
Fresh leg/uncured ham, boneless, barbecue at 285°F	3–4 lbs.	160º F	27–32 min. per lb.
Loin roast (boneless)			
New York (top loin)	2 lbs.	145–160ºF	20–26 min. per lb.
Pork roast	3–5 lbs.	145–160º F	12–15 min. per lb.
Pork loin center roast	2 lbs.	145–160ºF	20–26 min. per lb.
	3–5 lbs.	145–160ºF	12–15 min. per lb.
Sirloin pork roast	2 lbs.	145–160ºF	20–26 min. per lb.
	3–5 lbs.	145–160ºF	12–15 min. per lb.

Cut	Thickness/Weight	Internal Temperature (followed by 3-minute rest)	Average Recommended Cooking Time (minutes/pound or total)
Loin roast (bone-in)			
Ribeye (center rib pork roast)	2 lbs.	145–160ºF	22–32 min. per lb.
	3–5 lbs.	145–160ºF	14–17 min. per lb.
Sirloin pork roast	2 lbs.	145–160ºF	22–32 min. per lb.
	3–5 lbs.	145–160º F	14–17 min. per lb.
Ribs			
Pork back	1½–2 lbs. per rack	Tender	1½–2 hours
Country-style	3–4 lbs.	Tender	45 min. –1 hour
Spareribs (St. Louis–Style)	3½–4 lbs. per rack	Tender	1½–2 hours
Whole pork loin (boneless)	8–9 lbs.	145–160º F	8–9 min. per lb.
	10 lbs.	145–160º F	6–7 min. per lb.
Sautéing (add a little cooking oil to pan; sauté over medium-high heat and turn once, halfway through cooking time)			
Blade pork steak	¾ inch	145–160ºF	10–16 min.
Cutlets	½ inch	Tender	3–4 min.
Ground pork patties	½ inch	160ºF	8–11 min.
Ham steaks	½ inch	140ºF	6 min.
Loin chops (boneless)			
New York (top loin pork chop)	¾ inch	145–160ºF	8–12 min.
	1½ inches	145–160ºF	12–22 min.
Ribeye (rib) pork chop	¾ inch	145–160ºF	8–12 min.
Sirloin pork chop	¾ inch	145–160ºF	8–12 min.
Chops (bone-in)			
Porterhouse (loin) pork chop	¾ inch	145–160ºF	10–16 min.
Ribeye (rib) pork chop	¾ inch	145–160ºF	10–16 min.
Sirloin pork chop	¾ inch	145–160ºF	10–16 min.
Tenderloin medallions	¼–½ inch cubes	Tender	4–8 min.

Cut	Thickness/Weight	Internal Temperature (followed by 3-minute rest)	Average Recommended Cooking Time (minutes/ pound or total)
Braising (cook over medium-high heat in 1 tablespoon vegetable oil until browned evenly on both sides)			
Blade pork steak	¾ inch	Tender	11–12 min.
Cutlets	½ inch	Tender	3–4 min.
Loin chops (boneless)			
New York (top loin pork chop)	¾ inch	145–160°F	6–10 min.
Ribeye (rib) pork chop	¾ inch	145–160°F	6–10 min.
Sirloin pork chop	¾ inch	145–160°F	6–10 min.
Chops (bone-in)			
Porterhouse (loin) pork chop	¾ inch	145–160°F	8–12 min.
Ribeye (rib) pork chop	¾ inch	145–160°F	8–12 min.
Sirloin pork chop	¾ inch	145–160°F	8–12 min.
Loin cubes	1 inch	Tender	8–10 min.
Ribs			
Pork back	1½–2 lbs. per rack	Tender	1¼–1½ hours
Country-style	3–4 lbs.	Tender	30–35 min.
Spareribs (St. Louis–style)	3½–4 lbs. per rack	Tender	1¼–1½ hours
Tenderloin medallions	½-inch cubes	Tender	8–10 min.
Pork belly	2½–3 lbs.	Tender	40 min. per lb.
Pork shoulder roast	3–4 lbs.	Tender	30–33 min. per lb.
Arm (picnic)	5–6 lbs.	Tender	26–29 min. per lb.
Blade (Boston)	3–6 lbs.	Tender	2–2½ hours
Stewing (cook at a slow simmer, covered, with liquid)			
Cubes, loin or shoulder	1 inch	Tender	45 min.–1 hour

Source: National Pork Board, 2014

Note: Large cuts increase approximately 10°F while resting. Remove them from the heat at 150°F followed by a 10-minute rest. Doneness for some pork cuts is designated as "tender." Ground pork, like all ground meat, should be cooked at 160°F. The USDA recommends cooking pork chops, roasts, and tenderloin to an internal temperature between 145°F (medium rare) and 160°F (medium) followed by a 3-minute rest.

BAKED HAM

10- to 14-pound
   smoked or fresh ham

Glaze, optional

Preheat the oven to 300°F. Place the ham, fat side up, on a rack in an open roasting pan. Insert a meat thermometer so the point reaches the center of the thickest part. Be careful it doesn't rest in fat or on the bone. Do not add water. Do not cover. Roast until the meat thermometer registers 160°F. Allow 18 to 20 minutes per pound for roasting. About 20 to 30 minutes before the ham has finished baking, spread with a glaze, if desired, and return to oven to set the glaze.

HAM BAKED IN MILK

1 teaspoon dry mustard

¼ cup firmly packed brown sugar

1 slice of ham, 2 inches thick

Milk

Preheat the oven to 300°F. Mix the mustard and brown sugar in a small bowl and spread over the ham. Place in a small casserole dish. Add enough milk to barely cover the ham. Bake for 1 hour.

SPICED HAM LOAF

1 cup bread crumbs

½ cup milk

2 cups ground cured ham

½ pound ground fresh pork

1 tablespoon brown sugar

¼ teaspoon ground cloves

1 egg

Preheat the oven to 350°F. In a small bowl, soften the bread crumbs in milk. In a large bowl, combine the ham, pork, brown sugar, cloves, bread crumbs and milk, and egg. Mix and pack into loaf pan. Bake for 50 minutes.

PORK SPARERIBS AND SAUERKRAUT

1 quart sauerkraut

¼ cup firmly packed brown sugar

4 pounds pork spareribs

Salt and pepper

½ cup water

Place the sauerkraut in a greased baking dish and sprinkle evenly with brown sugar. Brown the spareribs under a broiler, sprinkle with salt and pepper to taste, and place on the sauerkraut. Add water, cover tightly, and bake at 350ºF for 1½ hours.

SMOKED PORK BUTT AND APPLES

2- to 3-pound smoked
pork shoulder butt

3½ cups plus 2 tablespoons
nonchlorinated water, divided

2 cups dried apples

3 tablespoons light brown sugar

½ teaspoon ground cinnamon

2 teaspoons lemon juice

2 tablespoons cornstarch

In a large pot, add 3½ cups water to shoulder butt. Cover tightly and simmer, allowing 30 to 40 minutes per pound. Turn once during cooking. About 40 minutes before the meat is done, add the apples. When the meat and apples are done, remove the meat. Add brown sugar, cinnamon, and lemon juice to the apples. Mix 2 tablespoons of water with cornstarch in a small bowl, then add to apples and continue cooking until thickened. Serve with meat.

PORK HOCKS WITH DRIED APPLES

2½ cups dried kidney beans

1 quart nonchlorinated water

3 pounds pork hocks

1 tablespoon salt

¼ teaspoon ground black pepper

1 tablespoon chopped onion

2 cups dried apples

Soak kidney beans overnight in 1 quart of water. Measure the water not absorbed by the kidney beans and add enough water to make 3½ cups. Brown the pork hocks on all sides in a dutch oven over medium-high heat. Season with salt and pepper to taste. Add the kidney beans, 3½ cups water, onion, 1 tablespoon salt, and ¼ teaspoon black pepper. Cover tightly and simmer 1 hour. Add apples and continue to simmer 45 minutes, or until done.

CHINESE PORK SHOULDER STEAKS

1 beef bouillon cube

⅓ cup hot water

1 teaspoon ground ginger

2 teaspoons salt

1 tablespoon sugar

¼ cup honey

¼ cup soy sauce

4 pork arm or blade steaks,
  ½- to ¾-inch thick

Dissolve bouillon cube in hot water. Combine ginger, salt, sugar, honey, and soy sauce in a large container. Marinate the steaks in the soy sauce mixture in the refrigerator for 2 hours or overnight, turning them occasionally. Remove the steaks from marinade and place on a rack in a roasting pan. Roast at 350°F for 1 hour.

CITRUS PORK TENDERLOIN

¼ cup flour

1 teaspoon salt

⅛ teaspoon ground black pepper

1½ pounds pork tenderloin,
  cut into 8 patties

3 tablespoons lard

11 ounces canned mandarin oranges

Preheat the oven to 325°F. Combine the flour, salt, and pepper in a shallow dish. Roll the tenderloin patties in seasoned flour until completely coated. Melt the lard in a skillet over medium heat, and then add the pork. Brown in lard and then pour off the drippings. Drain the mandarin oranges, reserving the liquid. Add liquid to tenderloin. Cover tightly and bake for 45 minutes. Top with mandarin slices before serving.

PORK ROLL-UPS

2 cups ground, cooked pork

¼ cup grated carrot

1 tablespoon minced green pepper

1 tablespoon grated onion

1 tablespoon salt

2 teaspoons soy sauce

¼ cup milk

For the pastry dough:

2 cups sifted white flour

¾ teaspoon salt

⅔ cup shortening

5 tablespoons nonchlorinated water

Grease a large baking pan. Combine ground pork, carrot, green pepper, onion, salt, soy sauce, and milk. Mix thoroughly.

For the pastry dough, mix the flour and salt together in a large bowl and blend in the shortening with a pastry cutter, a fork, or your fingers. Add water until mixture holds together.

Preheat the oven to 450°F. Roll out the pastry into a large 12 × 17 rectangle. Spread the pork mixture on pastry and roll up like a jelly roll. Cut into 12 rolls, 1-inch thick. Place the rolls in the greased baking pan and bake for 25 minutes, or until the pastry is lightly browned. Serve with a vegetable of your choice.

MANDARIN PORK SPARERIBS

2 to 3 pounds pork spareribs

½ cup soy sauce

½ cup orange marmalade

1 clove garlic, minced

½ teaspoon ground ginger

⅛ teaspoon ground black pepper

Saw the spareribs across rib bones so individual servings may be carved easily. In a large bowl, combine the soy sauce, marmalade, garlic, ginger, and pepper. Add the spareribs and marinate in the soy sauce mixture for 12 hours in the refrigerator, turning occasionally. When ready to bake, preheat the oven to 350°F. Place the ribs, rib ends down, on a rack in a baking pan. Cover tightly and bake for 1 hour. Remove the cover, turn the spareribs, and add half of the marinade. Bake for 15 minutes. Turn the spareribs again and add the remaining marinade. Bake for an additional 15 minutes, or until the ribs are browned.

CELERY PORK CHOPS

1 tablespoon lard

6 pork ribs or loin chops,
  ¾ to 1 inch thick

1 teaspoon salt

⅛ teaspoon ground black pepper

¾ cup chopped celery

2 tablespoons chopped onion

Melt the lard in a skillet over medium heat and add the pork. Brown in the lard, then pour off the drippings. Sprinkle salt and pepper over chops to taste. Add the celery and onion to the skillet, cover tightly, and simmer for 45 minutes.

STUFFED PORK CHOPS

6 pork chops, 1 inch thick

1½ cups whole-kernel corn

1½ cups bread crumbs

¾ teaspoon salt

¼ teaspoon ground black pepper

1½ tablespoons minced parsley

¾ teaspoon dried sage

1 tablespoon grated onion

1 cup diced apple

1 large egg

3 tablespoons milk

1 cup lard

¼ cup nonchlorinated water

Cut a pocket on the bone side of each chop. In a large bowl, blend corn, bread crumbs, salt, pepper, parsley, sage, onion, apple, egg, and milk together thoroughly. Stuff each chop with one-sixth of the mixture. Preheat the oven to 350°F. In an ovenproof skillet or pan, brown the chops in lard over medium heat. Pour off the drippings. Add ¼ cup water to the pan and bake, uncovered, for 1 hour.

PORK PIE

2 pounds pork shoulder butt

2 cups lard

2¼ cups boiling water

1 teaspoon salt

1 bay leaf

½ cup flour

2 cups cooked carrots

6 small cooked onions, sliced

For the pastry dough:

2 cups sifted white flour

¾ teaspoon salt

⅔ cup shortening

5 tablespoons nonchlorinated water

Preheat the oven to 325°F. Cut the pork into 1-inch cubes. Melt the lard in a dutch oven over medium heat, then add the pork and cook until browned. Add the water, salt, and bay leaf. Cover and bake until the meat is tender, about 1 hour. Drain drippings into a bowl and mix in flour to make a smooth paste; add cold water if needed. Add the paste back to the meat, along with the carrots and onions. Pour into a baking dish. Increase the oven heat to 450°F.

For pastry dough, mix flour and salt together in a large bowl and blend in shortening with a pastry cutter, a fork, or your fingers. Add water until mixture holds together. Roll out into a shape that will cover the top of a baking dish. Cover the meat in the baking dish with the pastry and bake for 20 minutes, or until the pastry is browned.

ROAST BOSTON-STYLE BUTT

1 4-pound Boston pork butt

½ cup light brown sugar

10 whole cloves

Preheat the oven to 350°F. Place the meat fat-side up on a rack in an open roasting pan. Season with salt and pepper to taste. Roast uncovered for 40 minutes per pound, or about 3 hours. Insert a meat thermometer into the thickest part, without touching bone. It should register 185°F when completely cooked. Thirty minutes before removing from the oven, sprinkle with brown sugar and stick with cloves.

FILLED CABBAGE

¾ cup rice

1 large cabbage (use only outside leaves; save center for salads)

½ pound lean ground pork

1 onion, diced

1 teaspoon salt

⅛ teaspoon ground black pepper

1 can (8 ounces) diced tomatoes

Soak the rice in cold water for 30 minutes. Drain and discard water. Place the soaked rice in a large saucepan with 2½ cups fresh water. Bring to a boil, cover tightly, turn heat to low, and cook for 25 minutes. Remove from heat and let cool.

Preheat the oven to 350°F. Bring a pot of water to boil. Blanch the cabbage leaves in the hot water for 3 minutes, then drain. Mix the pork, onion, salt, and pepper into the rice in the saucepan. Divide into as many servings as you'd like to have and roll each serving inside a cabbage leaf. Line a nonmetallic pan with extra cabbage leaves. Add tomatoes and cabbage bundles. Bake uncovered for 3 hours.

DINNER-IN-A-DISH

½ pound fresh pork steak

½ pound veal

¼ pound shell noodles

1 can (14 ounces) regular
chicken soup

¾ pound cheddar cheese, cut fine

½ green pepper, cut fine

½ small can pimiento, cut small

1 can (14 ounces) mushrooms

1 can (14 ounces) whole-kernel corn

1 cup buttered cracker crumbs

Cut pork and veal into 1-inch cubes. In a skillet heated with a little oil, brown
the meat and cook until tender. Cook the noodles in a large saucepan according
to package directions, drain, and add the meat. Add the soup and simmer for
5 minutes. Add the cheese, pepper, pimiento, and mushrooms with their juice.
Simmer for 10 minutes. Add the corn, stir lightly, and season to taste. Preheat the
oven to 350°F. Place in a casserole dish and cover with buttered cracker crumbs.
Bake until topping is browned.

PORK MILANESE

2 large eggs

1 cup Swiss cheese

2 cups fine bread crumbs

2 pounds pork steak, cut ¼-inch thick

4 tablespoons butter

Beat eggs slightly in a shallow bowl. Grate the cheese into a separate shallow
bowl and mix with bread crumbs. Dip each serving of meat into the beaten
eggs, and then in bread crumbs and Swiss cheese mixture. Melt butter in a
skillet and fry the pork in the melted butter. Turn only once.

POTATO AND PORK CHOP CASSEROLE

2 pork chops, 1 inch thick

3 medium potatoes, sliced

Salt and pepper

1 can (14 ounces) condensed mushroom soup

1 cup milk

Preheat the oven to 350°F. In a skillet heated with a little oil, brown the pork chops lightly. Arrange raw slices of potatoes in greased casserole dish. Season with salt and pepper to taste. Place pork chops on top and season to taste. Mix the mushroom soup with milk thoroughly and pour it over the chops and potatoes. Bake for 2 hours.

PORK SAUSAGE STUFFING

¾ loaf white bread

1½ cups boiling water

¾ pound pork sausage

⅓ cup onions, chopped

½ teaspoon salt

1 teaspoon dried sage

2 large eggs, beaten

Toast the bread, cut it into pieces, and add the pieces to a large bowl with the boiling water. Fry the pork sausage in a large skillet until brown. Add the onions and cook until soft. Drain the grease. Add the onions and meat to the bread, along with the salt and sage. When cool, add the well-beaten eggs. Return to the skillet and heat until the eggs are thoroughly cooked. Serve while hot.

SAUCY PORK 'N NOODLE BAKE

1 cup cooked pork, cubed

1 tablespoon lard

½ cup narrow noodles, uncooked

1 can (10½ ounces)
cream of chicken soup

1 can (8 ounces) whole-kernel corn,
undrained

1 tablespoon sliced pimiento

½ cup shredded sharp Cheddar cheese

¼ cup finely diced green pepper

Preheat the oven to 375°F. Brown the meat in melted lard in a skillet. When meat is well browned, drain the excess fat from skillet. Add noodles, chicken soup, corn, pimiento, cheese, and green pepper and mix well. Pour into 1-quart casserole dish. Bake for 45 minutes, stirring occasionally.

SPEEDY BACON AND BEANS

2 strips bacon, diced

1 small onion, minced

1 can (16 ounces) baked beans

½ teaspoon prepared yellow mustard

2 tablespoons chili sauce

Preheat the oven to 350°F. Sauté the bacon and onion until bacon is crisp and onion is yellow. Stir in the beans, mustard, and chili sauce. Pour into a greased 1-quart baking dish. Bake uncovered for 45 minutes, until the beans are brown and bubbling. (For variety, you can add 1 cup baked ham or slices of hot broiled or fried Canadian bacon.)

GLOSSARY

Aging: the time process involved that causes a maturing or ripening of meat enzymes that increase flavor and has a tenderizing effect.

Aitchbone: the rump bone.

Anterior to: toward the front of the carcass, or forward of.

Aspic: a jelly made from concentrated vegetable, meat, or fish stock, with gelatin.

Bake: to cook by dry heat in oven.

Barbecue: to roast meat on a grill, spit, over coals, or under a free flame or oven electric unit, usually basting with a highly seasoned sauce.

Barrow: a castrated male pig.

Baste: to moisten meat while cooking to add flavor and to prevent drying of the surface.

Boar: adult male pig kept for breeding purposes.

Boil: to heat to boiling point, or heat so as to cause bubbles to break on surface.

Bone-in cuts: meat cuts that contain parts of the bone.

Braise: a method of cooking meat in a small amount of liquid for tenderness and flavor.

Breed: a group of animals with common ancestors and physical characteristics.

Broil: to cook directly under heating unit.

Bulky feed: a feed that is usually high in fiber and lower in energy.

Butterfly: to split steaks, chops, and roasts in half, leaving halves hinged on one side.

Carcass weight: the weight of the carcass after all the butchering procedures have been completed.

Collagen: a fibrous protein found in connective tissue, bone, and cartilage.

Creep feed: a feed given to young pigs from 1 week of age to weaning.

Crossbred: a pig whose parents are of different swine breeds.

Cubed: cutting up meat into small square pieces.

Cure: any process to preserve meats by salting or smoking, which may be aided with preservative substances such as sodium nitrite.

Dam: female parent.

Dorsal to: toward the back of the carcass, upper or top line.

Dressing percentage: the proportion of the live weight that remains in the carcass of an animal, sometimes referred to as yield. It is calculated as: carcass weight ÷ live weight × 100 = dressing percentage.

Drippings: fat and juice from meat that collects in bottom of roasting pan.

Epimysium: the sheath of connective tissue surrounding a muscle.

Fabrication: the deconstruction of the whole carcass into smaller, more easily used cuts.

Farrow: to give birth.

Feed efficiency: the number of pounds of feed required by an animal to gain 1 pound in body weight.

Feeder pig: a young pig that has been weaned and is now ready to feed out, usually between 25 and 40 pounds.

Feeder pig sale: an auction where feeder pigs are sorted into uniform groups by weight and grade and then sold for public sale.

Fillet: to slice meat from bones or other cuts.

Finish: feeding a pig to market weight.

Forequarter: the anterior portion of a carcass, including several ribs.

Free choice: providing pigs with grain and a protein supplement in a self-feeder and letting them eat as they choose.

Freezer burn: discoloration of meat due to loss of moisture and oxidation in freezer-stored meats.

Fry: to cook in hot fat.

Full feed: giving a pig all it will eat.

Gambrel: a frame shaped like a horse's hind leg, used by butchers for hanging carcasses.

Gilt: a young female pig that has never farrowed or given birth to little piglets.

Glaze: to add luster to a food by coating with a syrup or jelly.

Grill: to cook food directly over an open fire or flaming coals.

Grind: to cut or crush in a food grinder.

Hindquarter: the posterior portion of the carcass that remains after the removal of the last rib.

Hog: a generic term that can be applied to a growing or mature pig.

Intoxication: when microbes produce a toxin that is subsequently eaten and sickness results in humans.

Lactic acid: an organic acid produced by the fermentation of lactose by certain microorganisms.

Lard: fat from pork.

Leaf fat: fat lining found along the abdominal wall in pork.

Length of hog: a measurement taken on the carcass or estimated on the live hog. It is the distance from the front edge of the first rib to the front end of the aitchbone.

Litter: offspring produced at one farrowing.

Live weight: the weight of the live animal at the time of purchase or the time of harvest.

Loineye area: the number of square inches in a cross-section of loineye muscle. This is taken by cutting the loin between the tenth and eleventh ribs and measuring the cut surface area of the muscle.

Marbling: fine streaks of white fat interspersed throughout the lean muscle of high-quality pork, beef, and lamb.

Marinade: an oil-acid mixture used to give flavor and sometimes to tenderize meats.

Marinate: to let food stand in oil-acid mixture for added flavor and sometimes tenderness.

Mince: to chop or cut into very small pieces.

Muscle pH: the acidity or alkaline level in the muscle. It generally declines after harvest, and the rate of decline is an important factor affecting meat quality.

Palatable: a feed that tastes good to the pig and is easily digestible.

Pan-broil: to cook uncovered in ungreased or lightly greased hot skillet.

Pan-fry: to cook in small amount of fat in skillet.

Perimysium: connective tissue covering and holding together bundles of muscle fibers.

Petcock: a small faucet or valve for releasing gas or air for draining.

Piglet: a newborn pig of either sex about 2 to 3 pounds and usually less than 8 weeks old.

Porcine stress syndrome (PSS): a term that covers a group of conditions associated with a recessive gene in pigs that causes acute stress and sudden death.

Posterior to: toward the rear of the carcass; behind.

Primal or wholesale cuts: the large subdivisions of the carcass that are traded in volume by segments of the meat industry.

Purebred: both sire and dam are from the same breed.

Rations: the diets formulated for pigs.

Render: to melt down the fat.

Retail cuts: the subdivisions of wholesale cuts or carcasses that are sold to consumers in ready-to-cook or ready-to-eat forms.

Rigor mortis: the progressive stiffening of muscles that occurs several hours after death as a result of the coagulation of the muscle proteins.

Roast: to cook, usually meats, by dry heat. Usually in oven, sometimes over open flame.

Runt: a small, undersized, or weak pig in the litter.

Salt pork: pork cured in salt, especially fatty pork from the back, side, or belly of a pig.

Sauté: to brown or cook in small amount of fat in skillet.

Sear: to brown surface quickly.

Shoat, shote: a pig of either sex after weaning, usually weighs less than 100 pounds.

Shrinkage: the weight loss that may occur throughout the processing sequence. It may happen due to moisture or tissue loss from both the fresh and the processed product.

Side: one matched forequarter and hindquarter, or one-half of a meat animal carcass.

Silverskin: the thin, white, opaque layer of connective tissue found on certain cuts of meats, usually inedible.

Simmer: to cook in liquid just below boiling point on top of range.

Sire: male parent.

Sow: female pig over 1 year of age that has farrowed a litter of pigs; rhymes with cow.

Stew: to cook slowly, covered by liquid, for a long time.

Stock: the liquid in which meat has been cooked.

Subprimal cuts: the subdivisions of the wholesale or primal cuts that are made to make handling easier and reduce the variability within a single cut.

Wean: to remove piglets from their mother; to take off milk.

Yield: the portion of the original weight that remains following any processing or handling procedure in the meat-selling sequence. It is usually quoted in percentages and may be cited as shrinkage.

METRIC EQUIVALENTS AND CONVERSIONS

Conversions between US and metric measurements will be somewhat inexact. It's important to convert the measurements for all of the ingredients in a recipe to maintain the same proportions as the original.

General Formula for Metric Conversion

Ounces to grams	multiply ounces by 28.35
Grams to ounces	multiply grams by 0.035
Pounds to grams	multiply pounds by 453.5
Pounds to kilograms	multiply pounds by 0.45
Cups to liters	multiply cups by 0.24
Fahrenheit to Celsius	subtract 32 from Fahrenheit temperature, multiply by 5, then divide by 9
Celsius to Fahrenheit	multiply Celsius temperature by 9, divide by 2, then add 32

Approximate Metric Equivalents by Volume

US	Metric
1 teaspoon	5 milliliters
1 tablespoon	15 milliliters
¼ cup	60 milliliters
½ cup	120 milliliters
1 cup	230 milliliters
1½ cups	360 milliliters
2 cups	460 milliliters
4 cups (1 quart)	0.95 liters
1.06 quarts	1 liter
4 quarts (1 gallon)	3.8 liters

Approximate Metric Equivalents by Weight

US	Metric
0.035 ounce	1 gram
¼ ounce	7 grams
½ ounce	14 grams
1 ounce	28 grams
16 ounces (1 pound)	454 grams
1.1 pounds	500 grams
2.2 pounds	1 kilogram

US	Metric
1 gram	0.035 ounce
50 grams	1.75 ounces
100 grams	3.5 ounces
500 grams	1.1 pounds
1 kilogram (1000 g)	2.2 pounds

Weight Conversion of Common Ingredients

1 pound salt = 1½ cups
1 ounce salt = 2 tablespoons
1 pound sugar = 2¼ cups
1 ounce cure = 1½ tablespoons

Conversion from Ounces to Tablespoons

¼ ounce = 1¼ tablespoons
½ ounce = 2½ tablespoons
¾ ounce = 3¾ tablespoons
1 ounce = 5 tablespoons
2 ounces = 10 tablespoons
3 ounces = 15 tablespoons
4 ounces = 20 tablespoons

Equivalent Measures and Weights

3 teaspoons = 1 tablespoon
4 tablespoons = ¼ cup
16 tablespoons = 1 cup
2 cups = 1 pint
4 cups = 1 quart
2 pints = 1 quart
4 quarts = 1 gallon
16 ounces = 1 pound

ACKNOWLEDGMENTS

I wish to acknowledge the support of my family: my wife, Mary, who has always been a good sounding board; Marcus, our son, whose photos appear here in his seventh book for Voyageur Press; and Julia, our daughter, who is always a bright spot in her father's life.

To Dr. Jeff Sindelar and Ronald Russell of the University of Wisconsin–Madison, who gave of their time and advice during photo-taking sessions.

To the Straka family of Plain, Wisconsin, for their assistance and patience while we acquired photos for illustrative purposes. For sixty-three years their family has served our local area, and I feel privileged to call them friends.

To Tony and Sue Renger of Willow Creek Farm, for allowing access to their pig operation for photos. Their attention to detail and providing quality pork products is an asset to our community.

To my good friends Jim Ruen and Wendy Wellnitz, for their support and understanding of what it takes to complete a useful book.

I also wish to thank my editor, Todd Berger, for all of his assistance in helping bring this book to a wide audience. Also, a thank-you to Caitlin Fultz for her attention to the manuscript and helping to strengthen it.

ABOUT THE AUTHOR

Philip Hasheider is a fifth-generation farmer who has combined his interests in production agriculture and history to write twenty-two books. *The Complete Book of Pork Butchering, Smoking, Curing, Sausage Making, and Cooking* is his ninth book for Voyageur Press. Others include *How to Raise Pigs; The Complete Book of Butchering, Smoking, Curing, and Sausage Making; The Hunter's Guide to Butchering, Smoking & Curing Wild Game and Fish*; and *The Complete Book of Jerky: How to Process, Prepare and Dry Beef, Venison, Turkey, Fish and More*. He is a three-time recipient of the Book of Merit Award presented by the Wisconsin Historical Society and Wisconsin State Genealogical Society and has written numerous articles for national and international livestock publications. He was the writer for the 2008 *Wisconsin Local Food Marketing Guide* for the Wisconsin Department of Agriculture, Trade, and Consumer Protection that received the 2009 Wisconsin Distinguished Document Award from the Wisconsin Library Association, and the national 2010 Notable Government Documents Award from the American Library Association. He lives with his wife, Mary, on their farm in south central Wisconsin where he continues writing. They have two children, Marcus and Julia.

INDEX